Casino Dictionary

GAMING AND BUSINESS TERMS

Casino Dictionary

GAMING AND BUSINESS TERMS

KATHRYN HASHIMOTO, Ph.D.

GEORGE G. FENICH, Ph.D.

Lester E. Kabacoff School of Hotel, Restaurant
and Tourism Administration
University of New Orleans

PEARSON
Prentice
Hall

Upper Saddle River, New Jersey 07458

Library of Congress Cataloging-in-Publication Data

Hashimoto, Kathryn.
  Casino dictionary : gaming and business terms / Kathryn Hashimoto,
George G. Fenich.—1st ed.
    p. cm.
  ISBN 0-13-171019-2
  1. Gambling—Terminology. 2. Casinos—Management. I. Fenich, George G.
II. Title.
  GV1301.H295 2005
  306.4'82—dc22

2005027595

Director of Development:
  Vernon R. Anthony
Senior Editor: Eileen McClay
Editorial Assistant: Yvette Schlarman
Executive Marketing Manager:
  Ryan DeGrote
Senior Marketing Coordinator:
  Elizabeth Farrell
Marketing Assistant: Les Roberts
**Director of Manufacturing
  and Production:** Bruce Johnson
Managing Editor: Mary Carnis
Production Liaison: Jane Bonnell

Production Editor: Donna Leik,
  TechBooks/GTS York, PA
Manufacturing Manager: Ilene Sanford
Manufacturing Buyer: Cathleen Petersen
Senior Design Coordinator:
  Miguel Ortiz
Cover Designer: Marianne Frasco
Cover Image: Eric Tucker, Getty Images
  Inc./Stone Allstock
Composition: *TechBooks/GTS* York, PA
Printer/Binder: R. R. Donnelley & Sons
  Company

This book was set in Times Roman by *TechBooks/GTS* York, PA. It was printed and
bound by R. R. Donnelley/VA. The cover was printed by R. R. Donnelley/VA.

Pearson Education LTD.
Pearson Education Singapore, Pte. Ltd.
Pearson Education Canada, Ltd.
Pearson Education—Japan

Pearson Education Australia PTY, Limited
Pearson Education North Asia Ltd.
Pearson Educación de Mexico, S.A. de C.V.
Pearson Education Malaysia, Pte. Ltd.

10 9 8 7 6 5 4 3 2 1
ISBN 0-13-171019-2

To Dante and Linda Laudadio, who took us in from Hurricane Katrina and gave us back our sanity. Thank you.

ABOUT THIS BOOK

Currently, the casino gaming industry is recognized as a viable career path by educators, researchers, policy analysts, and students. Further, the general public is also showing an increasing fascination with the subject. However, attempting to read and learn more about casino gaming can be as frustrating as a non-French speaker trying to understand a menu in a French restaurant: Many of the words and phrases seem to be in a foreign language. As with any industry, the jargon and buzz words make comprehension difficult.

This book solves the problem by defining the terms and language of casino management. Over 2,000 terms and phrases with unique uses or applications in the casino industry are defined and explained. Not only is this one of the most extensive compilations of terms used in this industry, but it goes a step further than other glossaries and dictionaries by including:

- Names and rules of the most popular games
- Gambling jargon
- Phrases used by dealers when referring to their bosses or their customers
- Types of cheating techniques
- Common terms and phrases used by managers in the casino departments of:

  marketing

  accounting

  economics

  finance

  management

  hotels and restaurants

No one with any interest in the casino gaming industry, whether casual or serious, can afford to be without this valuable resource.

ABOUT THE AUTHORS

Kathryn Hashimoto, Ph.D., worked in the hospitality industry for over ten years in marketing, sales, and training. Her first nine years of teaching were spent as a professor of marketing in business programs followed by another ten years teaching hospitality marketing, service management, and casinos. During this time, she became interested in gaming and presented over thirty papers on casinos. As a result of this research, Kathryn has testified before the Public Gaming Commission and the Rhode Island House Finance hearings on casinos. To develop a better understanding of casinos, she cofounded and organized a special interest section on gaming for the Council on Hotel, Restaurant and Institutional Education (CHRIE). She also worked with George Fenich on *Casino Management for the 90's* and *Casino Management: Past-Present-Future.*

To continue her research on gaming and to increase access to casino information, Kathryn cofounded the Association for Casino Education (A.C.E.), a nonprofit organization to disseminate information about the casino industry to educators and researchers, and to act as a link between industry and education. She also presents regularly at G2E (Global Gaming Expo) and has done consulting for Harrah's. Currently, she is writing and editing her third textbook in casino management. Kathryn is an associate professor at the Lester E. Kabacoff School of Hotel, Restaurant and Tourism Administration at the University of New Orleans.

George G. Fenich, Ph.D., spent over fifteen years as a hospitality industry practitioner before joining academia in 1985. He is currently a professor at the Lester E. Kabacoff School of Hotel, Restaurant and Tourism Administration at the University of New Orleans. George has done extensive research on the casino industry including work for the Casino Association of New Jersey. The results have been disseminated in working papers, academic journals, and conferences. He was instrumental in compiling the college text *Casino Management for the 90's.* Along with Kathryn Hashimoto, he helped establish the Casino Gaming Special Interest Section (SIS) for CHRIE.

George has also served hospitality education as a founder and commissioner of the Accreditation Commission for Programs in Hospitality Administration, as an officer and president of the Hospitality Educators of the Middle Atlantic Region, and as a member of the Board of Directors of CHRIE.

Casino Dictionary

GAMING AND BUSINESS TERMS

A

Abandon   To relinquish a hand or deal.

Above   Casino earnings as recorded in its bookkeeping ledger.

Absolute Advantage   Term in economics that refers to the ability of one firm to produce a good or service more efficiently than another.

Accountability   A person's ability to carry out assigned responsibilities and to be answerable for decisions.

Account Payable   An amount owed by the business.

Account Receivable   An amount owed to the business.

Ace   (1) A playing card. (2) In blackjack, a playing card with a value of one or eleven. (3) In craps, a single dot on one die. (4) One dollar bill.

Ace Adjustment   The adjustment for the proportion of aces remaining to be played in order to determine bet size.

Ace-Deuce   A throw of the dice totaling three.

Ace Poor   A lower than average proportion of aces remaining to be played, favoring the house.

Ace Rich   A higher than average proportion of aces remaining to be played, favoring the player.

Aces (Craps Two)   One die showing "one spot" up and the other die showing another "one spot" up.

A Cheval   In roulette, a bet on two numbers adjacent on the layout.

Across the Board   In racing, when a bettor places wagers on win, place, and show.

Action   Sum total of all wagers made on all gambling activity.

Action Plans   Specific plans that translate the service strategy into guides for employee activity over the coming period, usually a year.

Active Player   In baccarat, a player who represents a combined group of players in wagering against the bank.

ADA   An abbreviation for the *Americans with Disabilities Act.*

Addiction   A physiological and/or psychological dependency on one or more goods or services.

Adjusted Running Count   The value of the running count adjusted to reflect the number of aces rich or poor.

Administrative Principles   A branch of classical management theory concerned with identified principles of planning, organizing, commanding, coordinating, and controlling in an effort to manage the entire organization.

ADR   An abbreviation for *average daily rate*. One of the key operating ratios that indicates the level of a hotel's performance and is calculated by dividing the amount of dollar sales by the number of rooms sold.

Advertising   Any paid, nonpersonal communication transmitted through mass media by an identified sponsor.

Affirmative Action Programs   In a company, an agenda that enhances the organizational status of members of protected groups (e.g., minorities).

African Dominoes   Dice.

Agent   (1) An accomplice of a casino employee who poses as a player as part of a scheme to defraud the casino. (2) A person who takes lottery or numbers bets.

Aggregate Demand   Economic term referring to the total spending in a region as a whole over a given time frame, as in "The aggregate demand for gambling in Atlantic City is one billion dollars."

AH&LA   An abbreviation for *American Hotel and Lodging Association*.

AIDA   A marketing acronym for attention, interest, desire, action. It describes the functions that advertisements need to obtain: get attention, gain interest, and create desire to cause action.

A la Carte   (1) A menu on which food and beverages are listed and priced individually. (2) Foods cooked to order compared with food cooked in advance and held for later service.

All-Inclusive Package   A generic term for a package that includes all or nearly all the elements that travelers require for their trip, including airfare, lodging, food and beverage, ground transportation, taxes, and gratuities.

All Night Board Bingo   The card given to a player when he pays his admission, which is good for all games played during that session.

All Out   Pushing the limit to win, as in "She went *all out*, doing whatever it took to win the game."

Ambiance   The combined atmosphere created by the decor, lighting, service, possible entertainment (such as background music), and so on that enhances the dining or lodging experience.

Amenities   Features that add material comfort, convenience, or smoothness to a guest's stay.

American Plan (AP)   A billing arrangement in a lodging establishment under which room charges include the guest room and three meals per day.

American Roulette   Roulette wheel with two zeros, 0 and 00, with alternating black and red numbers that follow an ordered and symmetrical pattern with each odd number placed exactly opposite the next higher even number.

American Service   Food is dished onto individual plates and served to guests.

Americans with Disabilities Act (ADA)   Federal legislation passed in the 1990s that requires public spaces, including casinos, to be accessible and/or user-friendly to people with handicaps.

Amortization   In accounting, a product cost that is written off or paid down over a period of time longer than a year.

Anchor Man   In blackjack, the last player who is to the immediate right of the dealer.

Anchor Slot   In blackjack, the player in the first position; the same as first base.

Angle   (1) An idea. (2) A cheating method.

Ante   In a card game, a wager placed before the first card is dealt.

Any   In craps, the "any craps" wager.

Aperitif   A fortified wine flavored with one or more herbs and spices, usually consumed before a meal.

Apron   A place on the roulette table in which chips are stored by the casino when not in a tray.

Arm   A gambling operation backed or under the protection of organized crime, as in "the arm."

Around the Corner   A protocol in cards by which the ace is permitted to link the lowest and highest cards in a sequence such as queen, king, ace, deuce, two, and so on.

Arrival Date   In lodging, the day guests plan to appear with the expectation of a room being available for them.

Arrival Patterns   The patterns describing the number of customers arriving or entering a system in a given period of time.

Assets   Anything a business owns that has monetary value.

Atlantic City   A community in New Jersey, United States, where gaming was legalized in 1978 under strict regulations.

Atmosphere   The interior of a facility, the decor, or the atmosphere that is used to develop an image, differentiate the facility from its competitors, and draw customers.

Atmospherics   A consumer behavior term that refers to the use of space and physical features in a design to evoke certain effects in buyers.

Attack   When a gambler bets against the bank.

Attitudes/Opinions   The positive, neutral, or negative feelings a person has about macro issues regarding a company, institution, goods, services, the economy, politics, and so on.

Auction   In chemin de fer, the bidding that takes place in order to decide who will be the banker.

Audition   (1) A try out. (2) To deal for a supervisor with the hope of obtaining a job.

Authority   The right to take action and utilize business resources.

Authority Acceptance Theory   Chester Barnard's theory of what authority is and why people do, or do not, accept it.

Autocratic Leader   Someone who relies on direct commands and uses position authority as a management style with little input from others.

Autonomy   The degree to which the job allows individual freedom, independence, and discretion in such activities as scheduling work and determining task procedures.

Average Daily Rate (ADR)   In lodging, the occupancy ratio derived by dividing rooms revenue by the number of rooms sold.

Award Schedule   Printed schedule showing the payoffs and awards for a particular game or mechanical machine.

Ax   (1) When an employee is terminated or fired. (2) When the house takes its cut.

B

Baccarat   A card game made famous by fictional character James Bond in which players bet against a player who is called the banker, and a shoe is used to deal the cards; typically a high stakes game. Also called *chemin de fer, Nevada Baccarat, Punto Banco*, or *American Baccarat*.

Baccarat Banque   A version of baccarat found predominantly in France where the casino dealer acts as the banker, deals all cards, and banks all bets. Cards are dealt to two different players, each on either side of the table.

Back Counting   When someone who is not playing the table counts cards or counts down the deck. When a favorable count occurs, the back counter places their wager; usually done from a place behind the actual players at the blackjack table.

Backer Man   Also called the *bankroller*, it is the person who finances a game.

Backing Up Cards   (1) To prove a hand. (2) To move cards from one hand to another.

Back Line   In craps, the "don't pass" line.

Back Line Odds   With a bet on the don't pass line, a craps player lays odds on the point number.

Back of the House   The functional areas of the casino, hotel, or restaurant in which personnel have little or no direct contact with the guests.

Back-to-Back   Winning two hands in a row.

Back-to-Back Stud Poker   Two cards of the same denomination consisting of the hole cards and the first upcard.

Bad Debt   In accounting, the amount of money owed to the firm that is written off because it is uncollectible.

Badge   Slang term for a *gaming enforcement officer* or a *police officer*.

Bad Mouthing   The spreading of negative comments and opinions about an organization by a dissatisfied customer.

Bad Paper   In accounting, checks that are not honored at the bank.

Baggage   (1) A person who frequents a game but does not play. (2) A person who cannot pay his own expenses and expects someone else to do so.

Bagged   Arrested.

Balance Sheet   Financial statement identifying the assets and liabilities of an organization at a specific point in time.

Ball   The round, sphere-shaped object made to rigid standards of density and composition that is spun around the roulette wheel and, subsequently, falls into the winning slot number and color.

Ball Out   When the ball (see above) bursts out of the roulette wheel, invalidating the spin.

Bananas   Twenty-dollar chips used in baccarat that are yellow in color.

Banco   (1) Used in baccarat when a player wants to challenge the bank. (2) Term for the bank in chemin de fer. (3) Old-time cheating scheme.

Banco Suivi   In baccarat, a call by a player after she has lost a coup when she wants to bet against the bank again.

Bang Up   Closing the game or the house on command from a boss or supervisor.

Bank   (1) Sum of money present at a gambling table, also called the *bankroll*. (2) House or dealer who pays off. (3) Starting quantity of chips at the table.

Bank Craps   One version of craps in which the players wager against the house or banker and not against each other.

Banker   (1) An operator of a banking game. (2) A player who accepts bets from other players in a private banking game.

Bank Hand   One of two betting positions in baccarat.

Banking Game   Any casino game in which players bet against the house rather than each other.

Bankroll   In casinos, the amount of money the table is stocked with at the beginning of the shift.

Bankroll Man   The financier of a game.

Bar   (1) As in *to bar*; not allowed. (2) Barring twelve or two on "don't pass" bets allows the casino to accept "don't" bets. (3) Area where alcoholic beverages are served.

Barber Pole   A wager consisting of chips of various denominations and, thus, colors. When such a wager wins, chips are divided by color and paid by color.

Barriers to Competition   Factors that reduce the amount of competition or the number of firms, thereby allowing greater economic concentration to occur. Examples of barriers include legal barriers and regulatory barriers.

Barring the First Roll   A private craps hustler's bet in which a winning first roll for his opponent does not count, but is a "no decision" or standoff.

Base   (1) In blackjack, a player's betting position at the table. First base is the position farthest to the dealer's left, second base is directly in the center, and third base is the position farthest to the dealer's right. Second base is also called *center field*. (2) In craps, this refers to the position of the dealers. First base is the stickperson, second base is the dealer to the right of the boxperson, and third base is the dealer to the left of the boxperson.

Base Dealer   (1) A card mechanic who specializes in dealing off the bottom of the deck. (2) One of the dealers that deals from second or third base on a crap table.

Baseman   One of two dealers in the back of the crap game. The dealer books all line bets, field, come, don't come, place, lay, and buy bets.

Basic Strategy   (1) Elementary or nonadvanced approach to trying to win at a game. (2) Basic approach used by card counters in which memory in counting down the deck is not used.

Bean   A low value or one-dollar chip.

Bean Counter   An accountant.

Beanshooter   A cheating technique in which a simple holdout device is worn on the arm.

Beard   Someone who is used by the cheat to make bets for her because she is a known player.

Beat   (1) To overcome or beat the odds. (2) To cheat someone out of money in a gambling game.

Bed and Breakfast   A rate that combines a night's accommodation with a breakfast the following day. The breakfast can be either a full or continental.

Beef   An argument or complaint from a player against another player or the house.

Beefer   A complaining player.

Beliefs   People's ideas about the world around them and how it operates.

Belly Strippers   Cards that have been trimmed so that some of them are wider at the center along the sides than at the ends.

Benchmarking   In business, the search for the best practices among competitors that leads to their superior performance.

Bender   In cheating, a person who puts a very slight bend on the corners of cards so they can be identified later.

Benji   A one-hundred-dollar bill.

Benny Blue   In craps, a seven out.

Bernoulli System   A closed mathematical system in which each outcome has a constant probability of coming up, from one trial to another; the results of each trial are mutually exclusive of each other; each trial is independent of the other; and the sum of all possible outcomes is one hundred percent, such as in dice or roulette.

Bernoulli Theorem   The canon that decrees that the larger the number of trials within a system, the greater the likelihood that the actual results will approximate their mathematical expectation.

Best of It   When one player has a greater likelihood of winning than the other players due to a mathematical edge, greater skill, or through cheating.

Bet   A wager made by the player.

Bet Blind   A wager made without looking at one's cards.

Bet Both Ways   When the table has two-way action, betting on either the right or the wrong.

Bet the Dice to Win   Betting right that the shooter will pass.

Bet the Limit   Wagering the maximum amount that the table rules or the house allows.

Bet the Pot   A wager that matches the amount already on the table or in the kitty.

Betting Ratio   The mathematical relationship between the highest and lowest wager placed by a player.

Betting Right   In craps, a wager that the shooter will win.

Betting System   A series of mathematical rules that determine how a player should allocate his money among wagers on different trials in a game.

Betting Ticket   A computer form that is a player's receipt for a wager placed in race and sports.

Betting True Count   Varying bets based on the count, higher for "plus counts" and lower for "minus counts."

Betting Wrong   In craps, a wager that the shooter will lose.

Bevel (Beveled)   When dice have been modified such that one or more edges are slightly rounded rather than flat, so that the dice tend to fall on a certain number, thus improving the player's odds. Beveled dice are illegal.

Bicycle   The style used by a card manufacturer.

Big Bertha   In slots, oversized machines.

Big Con   Any elaborate con game or scheme lasting over several days and involving numerous people.

Big Dick   In craps, the point ten.

Big Order   Bookmakers phrase for a large bet.

Big Red   In craps, the number seven.

Big Six   Game that uses a large, vertical wheel with varied payoffs, often called the *Wheel of Fortune* or *Money Wheel*.

Big Six/Eight   A bet on six or eight in the corner of the craps table that pays even money.

Big Store   A fictitious establishment used in a big con that could be a gambling house, brokerage house, or bookmaking place in which the mark is led to believe she is going to swindle.

Bill   A gambler's term for a one-hundred-dollar note, as in "I lost five bills yesterday."

Bingo   Game where the goal is to match the numbers on a playing card to those drawn by the house using numbered balls. The standard winning pattern on the card is a complete list or line of numbers in a horizontal, vertical, or diagonal pattern. The game is a mainstay of Native American casinos and is not played in Atlantic City.

Bird   A loser or sucker who appears to enjoy giving his money away.

Bird Dog   An informant who provides hustlers with information on where they can find promising games or victims.

Bite   A request for a loan or credit, as in *to put the bite on someone.*

Black   (1) In roulette, a bet paying one to one. (2) A one-hundred-dollar chip.

Black and Whites   A term for the black pants and white shirts that dealers commonly wear.

Black Book   (1) A document put out by the Nevada Gaming Commission with the names and pictures of mobsters. If a casino allows entry of anyone listed, they can lose their gaming license. (2) A book with pictures and names of over twenty-five-hundred undesirables developed by an ex-lawman from Nevada. (3) A book of clients and their preferences kept by a prostitute.

Black in Action   When a hundred-dollar check is in play. This is an approval call by the floorman.

Blackjack   (1) Card game whose object is to collect cards that score twenty-one or less. (2) A hand comprised of an ace and a ten, or court card, valued at ten, to give a two-card total of twenty-one and a natural winner, but cannot be formed after splitting two aces. (3) What a gambler has when she beats the dealer, also called *BJ.*

Black Line Work   A cheating method in cards in which a small cut is made along the black line that borders each picture on a face card and is felt by the cheat as a means of identifying the card.

Blacklist   List and/or photographs of certain people who are not allowed in the casino.

Blackout Bingo   A winning setup in which a player must cover all twenty-four numbers on her card.

Blackout Work   A cheating technique in which the cards are marked by blocking out some of the design with white ink or some element of the design is somewhat embellished.

Blacks   One-hundred-dollar chips, usually black in color.

Blanket Roll   In craps, a controlled two-dice roll made on a soft surface, usually a blanket.

Blind Bet Poker   A bet made before the player looks at his cards.

Blister   A cheating method in cards in which a small bump is placed on the back of a card so the cheat can identify it whenever it is on the top of the deck.

Block   In lodging, a number of rooms set aside for members of a group, such as gamblers with comps.

Blood Money   Hard-earned money that one has difficulty attaining.

Blow   (1) To lose. (2) To be caught in the act of cheating.

Blower   The equipment used in keno or bingo to mix and select numbered balls.

Blowoff   Any technique for getting rid of a mark after she has been swindled in a con game.

Blueprint   A precise schematic diagram of a building, or part of a building, on which nonessential elements are eliminated, thus conveying information about the size, relative position, and distance of various parts.

Bluff   In poker, to bet heavily in spite of holding a weak hand in an attempt to make one's opponents think a good hand is held, with the expectation that opponents will drop out, allowing the bluffer to win.

Boards   (1) The raised element surrounding the table; also called the *rail* or the *blackboard*. (2) In Atlantic City, refers to the boardwalk when a player decides it is time to leave, as in *hit the boards*. (3) A group or commission that deals with policy issues occurring at the highest level of an organization (e.g., the Gaming Board).

Boat   Receptacle that contains the unused dice.

Body Language   Nonverbal body expressions that act as messages or impart additional information about the person or the verbal message.

Bond   (1) In human resources, the affiliation among organization members. (2) In finance, an interest-bearing certificate issued by a corporation or government, promising to pay interest and to repay a sum of money (the principal) at a specified date in the future.

Bones   Dice.

Book   (1) In lodging, to sell or reserve rooms ahead of time, for example, before the arrival date. (2) To supply the bankroll. (3) To finance a gambling scheme. (4) To accept a verbal wager on a casino game, especially in craps.

Bookie (Book, Bookmaker) (1) The person who collects and pays off bets for the house, both in and out of a casino. (2) An establishment or individual that accepts wagers on the outcome of races and sporting events, as in *Sports Book*.

Bookmaking The taking of bets on a specific event, such as a sporting event.

Book the Action Accept a wager.

Bop When a player jumps from table to table, often done in conjunction with partners at various tables who are card counters.

Bottom Dealer A cheating technique where the dealer draws cards from the bottom of the deck.

Bouleur Croupier who spins the roulette wheel.

Bouncer (1) Employee who is usually burly, keeps order in the house or bar, and ejects troublemaking patrons. (2) A check that cannot be collected.

Bowl In roulette, the wooden recess that holds the spinning part of the wheel.

Box (1) In craps, the receptacle or bowl in which the stickman keeps the dice. (2) In blackjack, a square area on the table in front of the player in which the bet is usually placed.

Boxcars In craps, to roll the number twelve.

Boxman (Boxperson) Casino employee in charge of the craps table who supervises the stickman or dealer, is subordinate to the floorman and pit boss, deposits money in the drop box, and monitors the payouts to ensure accuracy.

Box Numbers (1) A betting space on a money craps layout, nearest to the dealer, on which each of the possible point numbers (4, 5, 6, 8, 9, 10) appear within a square or box. Players may bet each or all of these numbers at any time. (2) The same as place bets in bank craps, and the same as off numbers in private craps.

Box Up (Box Them Up) Act of mixing the dice by the stickman so that the player may select another pair.

Boys (1) In craps, the dealers. (2) Players, gamblers. (3) Members of organized crime.

BP An abbreviation for *big player* or *high roller*.

Brainstorming In organizations, an idea-generating process that encourages alternatives while withholding criticism.

Branding Developing a mark, symbol, set of words, or combination of these to differentiate an organization from others.

Brand Loyalty   A pattern of repeat product purchases or uses, accompanied by an underlying positive attitude toward the brand, as in someone who always goes to Harrah's casinos.

Brass Buttons   Same origin as *cop*, meaning a police officer.

Break (Broke)   (1) A hand in blackjack that exceeds twenty-one. (2) Rest period for dealers, usually fifteen to twenty minutes in each hour worked (typically, dealers work cycles of an hour dealing followed by a twenty-minute rest period or break).

Break a Game   When one or more players end a game by winning all the money at a particular table or all the money the casino has.

Breakage   In craps, to allow more odds than what would actually be single, double, and so on of the flat bet to avoid paying multiple colors and cheating the player out of the change.

Break Down   To cut chips into countable stacks.

Break Even   (1) To win as much as one loses. (2) When revenues are equal to expenses.

Break Even Analysis   A managerial control aid that provides information on the required number of units or sales volume at which the business neither makes nor loses money.

Break In   (1) To get a dealer's job with little or no prior experience. (2) A new or novice dealer.

Break It Down   To cut chips into countable stacks or to segregate them by color.

Breaks   Luck, either good or bad, as in "Those are the breaks."

Break the Bank   (1) In European table games, the casino imposes a limit on the amount of casino chips supplied to each table. When the table loses its bank, it shuts down. (2) To win all a casino's money.

Break the Deck   In blackjack, to reshuffle the cards, usually in an effort to foil a card counter.

Brick   In craps, a cheating technique in which a die has been cut so that it is not true. See also *flats*.

Bridge   In cheating, to slightly bend the ten-cards lengthwise so that they are easy to spot on the table or in the deck.

Broke Money   A gift from the house of transportation costs to a player who lost all of his money. Also referred to as a *ding*.

Brush (The Brush)   (1) A cheating method in cards in which the perpetrator exchanges one of the cards in her hand for one from her accomplice's hand in the act of pushing the other player's cards aside on the table. (2) A cheating method in craps in which the cheat exchanges one pair of dice for another in the act of pushing the dice aside on the table.

Bubble Peek   A method of peeking at the top card of the deck by which the cheat catches a glimpse of one of the indexes of the card by buckling the front end of the card with his thumb.

Buck   (1) A one-dollar bill. (2) Machismo male.

Buck the Game   Bet against the house.

Budget   Guides the allocation of financial, human, and physical resources; often used in planning and control.

Buffet   In restaurants, a method of service in which the guests serve themselves. It includes a wide variety of items and is the "meal comp" provided to low rollers.

Bug   A device placed under the table or on the slot machine as a means of cheating.

Buildup   A scam that causes the cashier to return too much money when making change for a large bill.

Bull   Detective or police officer.

Bullet   Ace card.

Bum Move   Suspicious action by a player.

Bump Into   An action by the dealer in which she pushes a stack of chips next to and touching a shorter stack, and removes the excess to make both stacks equal.

Bum Steer   Incorrect or bad information.

Bundle   Large bankroll; a lot of money.

Bureaucracy   A system or organization and management characterized by specialization, a well-defined hierarchy, rules, impersonal regulations, and fixed criteria for promotion and selection, such as in government.

Burn a Card (Burned Cards)   (1) Removing one or more cards from the top of a deck and placing them face up on the bottom of the deck. Often done in blackjack or poker after the cards are shuffled. (2) After the cards that have been shuffled are put into the shoe, some of the first cards to come up are discarded.

Burned Out   (1) When a cheating method becomes so well known as to be useless. (2) Individual condition resulting from extended periods of stress and pressure.

Burnt Card   In single deck blackjack, a card that is reversed on the bottom of the deck to conceal it.

Burn Up   (1) An angry person. (2) Said of dice when they are making money passes.

Burr Dice   Dice in which the edges of some spots have been left with burrs so those sides will tend to catch if the dice are rolled on a cloth covered surface.

Burst   (1) In blackjack, cards totaling more than twenty-one. (2) Bust, break.

Business Travel Market   People traveling and dining out for business purposes and those attending conventions and meetings.

Bust   (1) In blackjack, cards totaling more than twenty-one. (2) Burst, break; worthless hand.

Bust Card   In blackjack, the nomenclature for the two, three, four, five, or six as the dealer's upcard because it is a difficult point to hit.

Busters   Misspotted dice.

Bust Hand   In blackjack, a hand totaling from twelve to sixteen. Also called a *hard hand*.

Bust In   To switch in misspotted dice.

Bust-Out Joint   A gambling house that follows a policy of cheating the players.

Bust-Out Man   A cheater who specializes in switching crooked dice.

Butterfly Cup   A dice cup that is modified in a way that allows the cheat to switch dice in the process of shaking them prior to rolling.

Buttons   (1) In roulette, the small markers used to identify the temporary value of a player's chips. (2) In craps, the small markers used to identify different types of bets. (3) Small markers used to record the amount of chips taken from a table without being paid for in cash or other chips.

Buy Behind   In craps, to purchase true odds behind a point number, wagering that the number will not be rolled before a seven, bought at a premium of 5 percent.

Buy Bet   In craps, a bet made on a point number, betting that the number will be rolled before a seven, with the bet usually bought at a premium of 5 percent of the amount of the bet and paid at true odds.

Buy In   In poker, the sum of money a player exchanges for chips. Also called *buying in*.

C

C & E   In craps, a split bet covering any craps and eleven.

Cackle   In craps, to feign the shaking of dice when, in reality, they are under control.

Cage   The highly controlled location of the casino cashier where transactions with players take place; operates like a bank.

Cage Credit   Player credit in currency or cheques issued at the casino cage after the completion of a marker or a counter check.

Calculators   Mathematicians, or odds men, who work in the calculations room at the racetrack.

Calibration Module   The part of the hard-count weight scale that provides for adjustment of the amount or number of coins to be counted.

Call   (1) The announcement of colors, numbers, changes, and wagers. (2) In poker, to end betting on a hand by covering the last gambler's wager without raising it.

Call Bet   A verbal wager that is made known by players and is illegal in New Jersey.

Caller   In keno or bingo, the person who runs the game by handling the numbers and calling out or posting those selected.

Call-in Numbers   Predetermined numbers representing the running count; adjusted for aces in counts that require a side count of aces and also used by the counter to summon a big player to his table.

Call Man   Casino employee who runs the baccarat game.

Call Plays   In blackjack, used by teams of card counters. It is a verbal signal to the player of the team by the counter of the team indicating how much to bet and how to play the hand.

Canadian Buildup   A short change sequence in which the hustler causes the cashier to hand over fifty dollars extra in the process of changing small bills for a large one.

Cane   In craps, the curved stick used by the stickman to reclaim the dice after each throw.

Canned Sales Presentation   All or part of the sales presentation is memorized to a standard formula.

Cannibalize   A situation in which one organization's brand takes customers away from one or more of the same company's other brands.

Canoe   In roulette, a numbered or winning section of a roulette wheel in which the ball finally comes to rest after the spin.

Can't Get to Him   Someone who is not tempted by a bribe.

Capable   Used in reference to a card or dice mechanic who does a good job of cheating.

Capacity Planning   A determination of the space needed to hold a given number of people or players.

Capital   (1) In finance, money needed for development. (2) Gambler's available money.

Capital Expenditures   A business's expenditures that are long-term investments in fixed assets such as a building.

Capped Dice   A cheating technique in craps by which the dice have been modified so that some sides are more rubbery or softer than others and favor certain numbers.

Capping Bets   (1) When the dealer pays off a bet by placing the payoff on top of the original wager. (2) Illegally adding chips to a wager after the game is in progress.

Capping the Deck   Adding palmed cards to the top of the deck.

Capture Rate   (1) A term used in hotel food and beverage to describe the number of hotel guests who use the food and beverage outlets. (2) Business term referring to the portion of a market that is controlled.

Card   (1) Basic device for many table games, including baccarat, blackjack, and poker, consisting of a stack or deck of fifty-two, made of laminated paper, and numbered on one side with a design on the other. (2) A funny person.

Card Counters   Intensely business-like players who closely track which cards have been dealt and adjust the size of their bets to reflect the extent to which the remaining cards are favorable or unfavorable to them.

Card Down   Expression directed to a floor person to indicate that a card has fallen off the table.

Card Eat   To spread to multiple hands in order to cause more cards to be dealt; usually done with small bets in minus counts.

Card Game   Games played with cards at a casino by which the casino receives a percentage rake-off or a timed buy-in from the operation of card games. In these cases, the casino is not a party to wagers.

Card Mechanic   A person who manipulates cards for cheating purposes.

Card Mob   Two or more card cheats working as a team.

Caribbean Stud Poker   This game is played on a twenty-one-type table and is based on five-card stud poker with the added attraction of a progressive jackpot.

Carousel   In a casino, the island of slot machines with one or more attendants in the middle.

Carpet Joint   A plush casino catering to high rollers.

Carre (Square Bet)   In roulette, a bet on four numbers whose boxes form a square on the table.

Carry a Slug   A cheating technique when a deck is shuffled without disturbing a particular group of cards, usually on the top or bottom.

Carte Blanche   (1) A player who has unlimited credit. (2) A hand of cards that contains no face cards.

Cartwheel   A silver dollar.

Case Bet   A wager that includes all the money or chips that a player has remaining.

Case Card   (1) The one remaining card in the deck that will improve a player's hand. (2) The last card of a suit or denomination still in the deck. (3) The last one of anything, as in *case note*; one's last dollar.

Case Study   A research design that produces in-depth, qualitative information based on one or a few organizations.

Case Stuff   Any cheating method that is not well known, even among professionals.

Case the Deck   To remember many of the played and exposed cards during the play of a game.

Cash Bank   An amount of money given to a cashier or server at the start of each work shift so she can handle the various transactions that occur. This person is responsible for the cash bank and for all cash, checks, or other negotiable instruments received during the work shift.

Cash Budgets   Financial aid, which contains estimates of cash receipts and cash expenditures for a period of time.

Cash Cow   A product or service that has a dominant position or a sizable market but limited growth potential, and which a company often uses as a cash subsidy for other products.

Cash Flow   Relates the amount and timing of revenues received to the amount and timing of expenditures made during a specific time period.

Cashier   The casino employee who handles transactions in the cage.

Cashier's Cage   The place in the casino in which transactions with players take place, is highly controlled, and where the cashier works.

Cash Out   Changing chips for currency.

Casing   Checking out or scouting the casino in preparation for some illegal activity, such as cheating or theft.

Casino   Establishment where betting is allowed and is legal, and which may or may not contain other amenities such as bars, food service, lodging and so on. Also called *house, joint, shop, store, toilet*, and *trap*.

Casino Administrator   Person responsible for the policies and procedures of the casino.

Casino Advantage   The percent advantage or edge that the house has over the player in any game.

Casino Checks   The chips that actually have a value printed on them and can be exchanged at the cage for money.

Casino Chips   Roulette chips of no value at the cashier's cage. These chips stay at the game and are exchanged for checks when the player leaves.

Casino Host   A casino employee who provides a personal service link between the casino and premium players.

Casino Hotel   A lodging facility that also contains gambling.

Casino Manager   Highest ranking person in the casino.

Casino Supervisor   Casino employee responsible for overseeing one or more table games and can include floor persons and pit bosses.

Catches   The numbers picked by a gambler that come up on the keno or lottery boards.

Catering   Part of the food and beverage division of a hotel that is responsible for arranging and planning food and beverage functions for conventions, smaller hotel groups, and local banquets booked by the sales department.

Catwalk   Concealed area, usually a walkway, above the casino floor used for observing play on the casino floor, where the objective is security.

Caught Up   When management determines that a player owes money and cannot pay it, thus no longer has credit, as in "They caught up with him."

CBD   An abbreviation for *Central Business District*.

CBX (PBX)   The telecommunications department.

Center Bet (1) In private craps, a wager between the shooter and the fader or faders that is placed in the center of the playing surface. (2) In bank or casino craps, another name for *proposition bets*.

Center Dealing A cheating technique where cards are dealt from the middle of the deck.

Center Field (1) In blackjack, the center box or position directly across from the dealer. (2) In craps, the field bet nine.

Central Business District (CBD) The hub of business activity in a community, which includes offices and retailers.

Central Credit A credit-reporting agency that provides information on the credit history of casino customers who have applied for or have been granted casino credit.

Centralization In business management, the extent to which decision authority and responsibility rests with few, rather than many, organizational members, usually high-level managers.

Central Limit Theorem The statistical rule that, as the sample size is increased, so the sampling distribution approaches the normal distribution form and serves as the basis for craps.

Central Processing Unit A phase computing system in which data is processed based on programmed instructions.

Central Reservation System Allows guests to call one phone number to reserve a room at any of a specific chain's properties.

Century One hundred dollars.

CEO An abbreviation for *Chief Executive Officer*.

CF An abbreviation for *control factor*.

Chain of Command In management, an unbroken hierarchy of authority linking superiors and subordinates in an organization.

Chance Statistical probability.

Change Agents (1) On the casino floor, those who exchange cash as a service to players. (2) In an organization, people who act as catalysts and manage the change process.

Change Attendant Casino employee who has a casino-issued bank used to make change for slot customers.

Change Colors To exchange one denomination of casino chips for another, thus changing the color of one's chips.

Change Only A call in the craps game to signify that the money thrown in by the player is not a bet; it is specifically for change.

Change Up (Color Up)   To change one denomination of chips for the next higher denomination, thus substituting colors.

Channel   The medium through which a message travels.

Charismatic Leadership   Followers make attributions of heroic or extraordinary leadership abilities when they observe certain behaviors in managers or owners; often attributed to the movers and shakers in the casino industry.

Charter Bus   In casinos, the bus program the casino or hotel arranges or leases.

Chase   In stud poker, to play against a superior hand that is exposed.

Cheat   Bottom dealer, also called a *mechanic*.

Check (Checks)   Casino chips that are nonmetallic gaming tokens used in place of currency in the casino and come in various denominations ranging from one to five thousand dollars:

$1.00	white
$2.50	pink
$5.00	red
$20.00	yellow
$25.00	green
$100.00	black
$500.00	purple
$1,000.00	orange
$5,000.00	gray

Check Change   Changing higher denomination checks for lower denominations.

Check Cop   (1) An adhesive paste that a cheat places on her palm. When she puts her hand on a stack of checks or coins, the top one adheres to her palm and she steals it. (2) Stealing chips out of a poker game.

Check Copping   Stealing chips off the table, either from other players or the pot.

Check Down   Expression directed to a floor person when a chip or money drops to the floor.

Checker   Casino employee who monitors the shills to determine how many players they bring to the game.

Check Out   (1) To observe or analyze something or someone. (2) In lodging, the procedures involved in the departure of a guest from the property, including settlement of the guest's account.

Checkout Sheets   Counts sheets used by cashiers in the casino to balance their banks at the end of the shift.

Checks Play   Any bet over fifty dollars that is announced to the floorperson.

Chemin de Fer   A form of baccarat in which the players compete among themselves and not against the house; common in Nevada.

Cheque   A negotiable gaming chip that has a specified value and can be used throughout the casino or redeemed for cash. The term is used interchangeably with the term *chips*.

Chicken Feed   An insignificant quantity of money; small change.

Chief Executive Officer (CEO)   The highest, top-level manager in an organization.

Chief Information Officer (CIO)   A senior level manager whose major role is to oversee information as a resource in strategic, tactical, and operational planning.

Chief Operating Officer (COO)   The highest-ranking employee who is responsible for day-to-day operations and ranks below the CEO.

Chill   To lose interest.

Chip   (1) Token used instead of cash on all gaming tables and used to mark a bet. (2) A gambler with a lot of money. (3) The small electronic device that contains the computer program found in a slot machine; made of etched silicon.

Chip Cup   A cheating technique that uses a stack of simulated chips, which is actually a hollow cup and is used to steal chips from the casino.

Chip Float   The dollar value of chips or cheques that are held by customers. Float is also calculated for slot tokens.

Chippy   (1) An inexperienced player. (2) A sucker.

Chiseler   (1) A gambler who tries to pick up another player's bet in a banking game. (2) A gambler who borrows money in a private game and doesn't repay.

Chi-Square Test (X^2) A test statistic that allows one to decide whether observed frequencies are essentially equal to or significantly different from frequencies predicted by a theoretical model. The outcome of the test is used to determine whether or not frequencies are distributed equally among categories, whether or not a distribution is normal, or whether or not two variables are independent.

Chuck-A-Luck   A game of chance where three dice are spun in an hourglass-shaped wire frame called a *chuck cage* and a *betting layout*. Also called *Nevada Chuck-a-luck, Grand Hazard*, or *Hazard*.

Chump   A sucker, chippy, mark, monkey, pheasant, bird, or greenie.

Chunk   To regularly make large bets or too large a bet.

Cinch Hand   In poker, a hand that is sure to win the pot.

CIO   An abbreviation for *Chief Information Officer*.

Circled Game   Situation in which the sports book reduces the normal betting limit on a game.

Claim   A player trying to get paid for a winning bet that he did not wager.

Claim Bet Artist   In cheating, a person who generally claims bets around dice tables, in which players can lose track of their bets.

Claimer (Collector)   In a slot cheating scam, the person who has responsibility for collecting the jackpot.

Clapper   The item that hangs in a vertical position at the top of the big six wheel. It is often made of leather, rides on the top of the pegs, and determines the winning number when the wheel stops.

Classical Decision Model   In economics, a decision-making approach that assumes individuals make decisions based on rational and unemotional thinking.

Class I Gaming   Traditional Indian games; low-level games played only by tribal members. These games are completely under tribal law and not subject to state or federal jurisdictions.

Class II Gaming   Bingo, certain card games, and video displays of those games; controlled by Indian tribe and the federal Indian Gaming Commission.

Class III Gaming   A class of gaming created by the Indian Gaming Regulatory Act that includes most casino games. For a state to have Class III gaming, gaming must be legalized for commercial (non-Indian) gaming operators and must be conducted in conformance with a contract or agreement between state governments and the tribes.

Clean   To take all of the money a player has.

Clean Hand   An empty hand that can be shown not to contain palmed cards or dice.

Clean Money   Checks taken from the dealer's rack or tray for payment purposes.

Clean Move   A well-executed cheating action.

Clear   (1) Not guilty of cheating. (2) Free of debt.

Clip   Cheat.

Clock   To keep track of the amount of money won and lost during a game.

Clocker   One who clocks a banking game.

Clock In   When a casino employee who is paid on an hourly basis arrives at work or departs and has his time slip record the hour.

Clocking   Keeping track of action, such as the number of hands dealt or the number of spins taken on a big six wheel, during a given time period.

Closed Cards   Cards dealt face down.

Closed-Ended Question   A survey question that offers respondents a set of answers from which they are asked to choose the one that most closely reflects their views.

Closer   The form left in the tray at closing that designates the value of the tray or inventory.

Closer Card   A two-part document used to record the table inventory at the end of each gaming shift.

Close to the Belly (or Vest)   A stud poker player who bets only on a wired pair or when he has the best hand showing; is playing "close to the belly."

Club   An association of persons with a common objective, usually jointly supported and meeting periodically.

C-Note   One-hundred dollar bill.

Cocked Dice   In craps, when one or more dice stop on some surface other than the felt and, thus lie at an angle that makes it difficult to determine which die surface is pointing up.

Coercive Power   In management, the ability of a leader to administer punishment to subordinates, thus gaining power through fear.

Cognette   In baccarat, a slot in the table reserved for the bank's winnings or cut of winnings.

Cognitive Dissonance   Postpurchase doubt; a feeling of anxiety that a buyer experiences after making a purchase.

Cohesiveness   In groups, particularly certain departments of a business, the strength of interpersonal attraction among members and the degree to which they are motivated to remain part of the group.

Coin-in   The amount of coins actually inserted into the coin slot or played off of the credit meter. Each machine has multiple electronic meters that are used to monitor the operation of the slot machine.

Cold Deck   (1) A deck or shoe unfavorable to the player. (2) A cheating technique by which the deck of cards has been arranged in a certain order for purposes of switching later for the deck in play.

Cold Dice   Dice that are not making the player's point.

Cold Player   A gambler who is on a losing streak or a run of bad luck.

Cold Turkey   When the first two cards that are dealt are face cards.

Collective Bargaining   Process of negotiating a union contract and of administering the contract after it has been negotiated.

Collector   The participant in a slot cheating scam whose job is to actually claim the jackpot; see also *claimer.*

Collusion   (1) Cooperation between two individuals for mutual gain. (2) Agreement between different firms to cooperate by raising prices, dividing markets, or otherwise restraining competition.

Color   Designation of the value of chips by their color.

Color Change   Changing one color of checks for another color of higher denomination checks.

Color for Color   Expression used by dealers when they pay out a bet by matching each denomination of chip wagered.

Color Up   A transaction by which the player exchanges cheques for an equivalent amount of a higher denomination of cheques.

Column Bet   In roulette, a bet on twelve vertical numbers on the layout. The winning unit is paid off at two-to-one odds.

Combination Bet   In roulette, a bet on more than one number using a single chip.

Combinations   Syndicate of gamblers.

Come Bet   In craps, the same as a pass-line wager.

Come-Out Bet   In craps, a bet made on a specific number or group of numbers that the number or one of the group will be thrown on the next roll of the dice.

Come-Out Roll   In craps, the first roll after a pass-line decision that establishes the point.

Come Up   A chance or number *comes up* when it wins.

Coming in One High   A cheating technique used by a dealer to short a player on the payoff by secretly transferring a chip from the player's wager to the payoff stack.

Coming Out   In craps, when the stickman informs the players that the dice are ready to be thrown, which is a warning that all bets must be placed immediately.

Commission   A percentage or fee charged by the casino on some bets or games and monitored by the dealer using plastic markers or lammers placed in a specific area of the layout that correspond to the player's numbered seats. In baccarat, it is 5 percent.

Comp(s) Short for *complimentary goods or services* given to players and can apply to things as low cost as drinks to full room, beverage, and transportation costs. They are a marketing tool used to attract players to a certain casino and are also called *full comps* (room, food, beverage).

Comparative Advantage An economic term that says a firm, nation, or region should specialize in producing commodities that it can produce at relatively lower costs than others.

Compensation All of the direct and indirect pay that an employee receives for the job performed.

Competitive Advantage A term used in economics to describe the distinct competency one entity has over its competitors. These competitors can include businesses, communities, regions, and so on.

Compulsive Gambler A progressive behavior disorder in which an individual has an uncontrollable urge to gamble.

Concierge An employee whose basic task is to serve as the guest's liaison with both hotel and nonhotel attractions, facilities, services, and activities.

Confidence Interval A measure that specifies the range of values within which a given percentage of the sample mean falls.

Conflict Perceived incompatible differences that result in interference or opposition.

Connected Having association with organized crime.

Console A flat-top, electrically powered slot machine that can be played by one or several players simultaneously.

Conspicuous Consumption The purchase and prominent display of luxury goods to provide evidence of a consumer's ability to afford them; often attributed to high rollers.

Construct Validity A process that involves relating a measuring instrument to a general theoretical framework in order to determine whether the instrument is tied to the concepts and theoretical assumptions that are employed.

Consumer Behavior The process by which individuals decide what, when, where, how, and from whom to purchase goods and services.

Content Theories Theories developed by Maslow and Hertzberg that describe the various factors, or content, that affect human motivation.

Continental Breakfast A small meal at the start of the day that usually includes a beverage, rolls, butter, and jam or marmalade.

Contingency Plans In management, predesigned actions for meeting certain possible conditions.

Contract Bet   In craps, a bet that may not be removed or reduced once a point has been established. Pass line and come bets are contract bets.

Control   The process of monitoring activities to ensure they are being accomplished as planned and of correcting any significant deviations.

Controller   Head accountant who manages the accounting department and all financial dealings of the business.

Convention   (1) Generic term referring to any size business or professional meeting held in one specific location, which usually also includes some form of trade show or exposition. (2) A group of delegates or members who assemble to accomplish a specific goal.

Convention and Visitor Bureau (CVB)   An organization, typically nonprofit, that is responsible for marketing a specific destination.

Convention/Meeting Planners   Persons who plan and coordinate meetings and conventions.

Conversion Factor (CF)   In card counting, the number by which the running count is divided, sometimes multiplied, to derive the true count; generally equal either to the number of full decks or half decks that have not been put into play.

COO   An abbreviation for *Chief Operating Officer.*

Cooler   A prestacked deck that is secretly switched for the deck in play.

Cooler Move   A sleight of hand technique for exchanging a prestacked deck for the one in play.

Cool Out   To calm down a mark who has been swindled in order to keep him from causing problems.

Cop   (1) To get, take, or steal. (2) To win a bet.

Core Values   A set of important values that seems to define a specific organizational culture and is important with regards to how society views gambling.

Corker   An unusual player, either good or bad.

Corner Bet   In roulette, a wager placed on the intersection of four numbers that is paid at eight to one; also called a *square bet.*

Corner Red   Big six/eight.

Corporate Culture   Governs how people relate to one another and their jobs; the overall feel or style of a company.

Corporation   A business firm formally incorporated under state law, which thus, separates the company from its owners or stockholders and also limits owners' liability.

Correlation Analysis   A statistical process that estimates to what extent variables are related to one another.

Count   (1) The act of tallying the chips in a tray or the proceeds from a drop box. (2) The cumulative value of all cards played at any given time.

Count Down   An action by a dealer to make small, regulation-sized stacks of chips from taller ones so that they can be easily counted from a distance.

Counter   In blackjack, a card counter.

Counter Check   A draft used to secure credit or markers.

Counter Magnet   An electromagnet built under a bar or store counter on a craps table to control metallically loaded dice.

Count Room   A secure, tightly controlled room or office in which casino receipts are counted at the end of each gambling session.

Coup   In European casinos, the term for a complete round of play in games such as baccarat or roulette.

Court Cards   The jack, queen, or king, all of which have a value of ten in blackjack and zero in baccarat.

Cover   (1) To place a wager on a table. (2) To accept a bet. (3) Each meal served.

Cover All   In bingo, a winning position on a card in which all twenty-four numbers have been called and covered.

Cover Bet   A bet made by a counter to disguise from casino employees that he is counting.

Covered Square   In bingo, the center square in the N column of a bingo card; it has no number and is considered a free play.

Cover Play   A play of the hand; usually a strategy error made by a counter to disguise from the casino employees that he is counting.

Covers   The guest count of a restaurant.

Cowboy   A fast or brash gambler.

CPU   An abbreviation for *central processing unit.*

Crap Out   In craps, to roll a two, three, or twelve on the first roll and lose.

Craps   (1) Table game using two dice, each with spots representing the numbers one through six. (2) In the game of craps, when a two, three, or twelve are rolled.

Craps Crew   Four dealers assigned to a single craps game.

Craps Dealer   A casino employee who is in charge of the collection and payoff of wagers.

27

Crap Shoot (Craps Shoot)   Any venture in which the result is unknown and, thus, is a gamble.

Craps Hustler   A player who takes advantage of novices by placing craps bets at less than correct odds.

Credit   (1) The custom in casinos by which gamblers are allowed to bet without money if they agree to repay all losses they might incur. (2) In accounting, an entry on the right side of an account.

Credit Limit   The maximum amount of credit that casino management authorizes a player to receive.

Credit Manager   Casino employee who determines how much credit to allow a given player.

Credit Play   Wagering based on the issuance of credit and documented by the completion of a credit instrument (marker).

Credit Slip   Voucher or printed form that, when completed, accounts for the value of chips taken away from a table.

Crimp   A cheating move in which the corner of cards are bent so they can be identified later.

CRM   An abbreviation for *customer relations manager.*

Cross   A brief con in which the victim is led to believe she is going to be partners with a cheat in swindling a card or dice game.

Cross-Fill   The transfer of cheques from one table game to another; prohibited in most gaming jurisdictions.

Cross Firing   Dealers talking to each other on a live game about things that are not game related.

Crossroad   Cheats who specialize in swindling the casino from the outside.

Cross Training   Enables employees to learn the tasks associated with more than one job and, thus, fill in when necessary.

Croupier   A French word or term for gaming table employees.

Cubes   Dice.

Cucumber   An especially inexperienced, green, or novice sucker.

Cull   Cheating technique in cards in which certain cards are sorted out of the deck for later use.

Culture   A group of people sharing a distinctive heritage or background, such as *corporate culture.*

Cup   Container in which dice are shaken; often made from leather.

Curator   In baccarat, the player whose turn it is to deal.

Curbside Appeal   Visual appeal and cleanliness designed to encourage people to dine in a particular restaurant.

Currency   Coins and paper money.

Currency Acceptor   A device that allows the slot machine to accept currency; a *bill validator*.

Current Assets   A financial term for organizational resources that can be converted to cash relatively easily.

Current Ratio   A financial liquidity concept that compares current assets to current liabilities.

Cushion   Reserve bankroll.

Customer Deposits   Money deposited with the casino cage for the purpose of wagering; also known as *front money*.

Customer Relationship Management   A business strategy to select and manage customers to optimize long-term value by creating personal connections.

Customer Service   A management term referring to the policies set by the corporation and the extent to which the employees may go to satisfy the customers.

Cut   In card games, splitting the deck into two piles and putting them back together in a different order; signifies an unbiased shuffle.

Cut a Line   To divide the proceeds of a gambling scam equally between two or more people.

Cut Card   A divider; usually a solid piece of plastic put into the deck or the shoe to designate when the cards will be shuffled next.

Cut Cheques   When a dealer holds a stack of chips in one hand and uses his index finger to create a series of equal stacks; also called *thumb cut* or *drop cut*.

Cut Edge Dice   A method of cheating in which the edges of each die are cut or shaved to larger and smaller angles so the dice fall in the direction of the larger cut.

Cut In   A cheating technique in craps in which other dice are switched for those in play.

Cut Into   Matching a stack of a certain color of chips with another stack of the same color.

Cutout Work   A cheating technique in cards in which a small part of the white section of the back design is extended with an acid or a knife that removes the ink, thus adding white area that was not there originally.

Cutter (1) In poker, an employee who takes a percentage of money out of the pot to pay for the gambling facilities. (2) In baccarat, the dealer takes a 5 percent cut from the banker's winning bet.

Cut Tokes To divide the tips or gratuities among the dealers.

Cut Up Jackpots To openly discuss previous large wins that are usually exaggerated.

CVB An abbreviation for *Convention and Visitor Bureau.*

D

Data Facts that have yet to be processed or organized for meaningful use.

Database In computers, a collection of retrievable information.

Daub A cheating move in which cards are marked with coloring to facilitate later identification.

Days Expression used by casino employees to refer to the work shift that occurs during daylight; usually starts between 7 a.m. and noon.

Day-Trip Market A market segment that can drive to the property and return home the same day.

DB An abbreviation for *debit.*

Dead Head (1) A patron who is out of money. (2) A nonplayer. (3) In Atlantic City, when a casino bus returns to the point of departure without the original passengers.

Dead Man's Hand A poker hand containing aces and eights; purported to be the hand held by Wild Bill Hickock, legendary gunfighter and lawman, when he was shot dead playing poker in Deadwood, South Dakota.

Dead Number Dice In craps, a cheating technique in which dice are modified or loaded in such a way that one number comes up more often than statistically determined.

Dead Table Table to which a dealer is assigned but has no players.

Deadwood Players People who loiter in the casino but do not play, often due to lack of resources.

Deal Around When a dealer deliberately avoids giving cards to a player, often because the player is intoxicated.

Dealer Casino employee who conducts a table game but does not necessarily deal cards; also called the *croupier.*

Dealing a Blister   Top deal seconds in connection with a deck of cards in which certain cards have actually been marked. The cheat can feel when a desirable card is on top of the deck and she holds it back for herself or a partner by second dealing.

Deal Out   (1) The act by the dealer of getting the cards to the players. (2) To exclude a player from the game.

Debit (DR)   In accounting, an entry on the left side of an account.

Decentralization   A management term referring to decisions being made at the local/unit level rather than the corporate office level.

Deferred   Understanding that the commission or "vigorish" will be paid later.

Delegation   In management, the process of assigning tasks and responsibility and granting authority to ensure that those tasks are accomplished.

Delivery   Manner of getting the cards to the players.

Delphi Technique   A qualitative forecasting tool; a formal process that involves surveying experts combining or averaging their individual forecasts, followed by another round of estimates based on a sharing of the individual and combined forecasts to arrive at a final combined forecast.

Demographics   Objective and quantifiable population statistics that are easily identifiable and measurable (age distribution, income, etc.).

De Moivre Theorem   The rule that, during a series of trials within a Bernoulli system, the actual results will fluctuate from the mathematically determined result in direct proportion to the square root of the number of trials.

Denomination   The value or rank of a card, chip, or cash.

Departmentation   In management, the process of grouping activities or tasks into an organizational unit to accomplish some common purpose, such as the accounting department.

Dependent Variable   Variable that the researcher wishes to explain.

Depreciation   An estimated measure of the value lost to an asset over a period of time; often established by the Internal Revenue Service.

Descriptive Statistics   Statistical procedures used for describing and analyzing data that enable the researcher to summarize and organize the data in an effective and meaningful way and provide tools for describing collections of statistical observations and reducing information to an understandable form.

Destination Management Companies   A professional services company possessing extensive local knowledge, expertise, and resources, and specializing in the design and implementation of events, activities, tours, transportation, and program logistics.

Destination Market   A market segment that stays overnight, usually as a vacation.

Deuce   (1) Two dollars. (2) The two-spot on a die. (3) In cards, the two.

Deuce Dealer   A dealer who specializes in dealing seconds.

Dice   The plural of die; refers to the two objects that are played with in craps, each having six sides with spots representing the numbers one to six.

Dice Are Off   Dice that are not "true," either from use or in an effort to cheat.

Dice Boat   A container on the game table that retains the dice that are not being used.

Dice Chute   A plastic tube used to drop the dice in some games; designed to reduce the possibility of cheating through the use of a cup or throwing by hand.

Dice Degenerate   Compulsive craps players who cannot control their need to gamble.

Dice Picker   In craps, the casino employee who retrieves dice that have fallen or been thrown off the table.

Die   Singular of dice; a small cube with six sides with spots representing the numbers one to six.

Differentiation Strategy   The approach a firm follows when it wants to be unique in its industry along dimensions widely valued by buyers.

Dime   Wager of one thousand dollars.

Direct Costs   Expenses incurred by a firm that are in proportion to the output of a good or service.

Direct Marketing   The process of attempting to reach the market directly through such media as mail or telephone.

Dirty Money   (1) Chips from losing wagers that have not been returned to the bankroll. (2) Money obtained through illegal means.

Discard   (1) Playing card that is removed from the deck until the next shuffle. (2) Used cards.

Discard Holder   Receptacle, usually metal or plastic, that is used to retain the discarded cards.

Discard Tray An area in which used cards are stored until they are shuffled; used primarily in blackjack and baccarat.

Discipline In business, actions taken by a manager to enforce the organization's standards and regulations.

Discretionary Income An individual's or family's money that is left over after paying taxes and buying necessities.

Disposable Income Roughly, take-home pay or that part of total income that is available for consumption or saving.

Diversification A business strategy of adding products or services areas to the organization that are different from the current ones provided.

DMC An abbreviation for *Destination Management Company.*

Dollar A wager of one hundred dollars.

Dolly In roulette, the cylindrical object, usually glass, which is used to designate the winning number.

Domain The market and the products or service areas in which the organization intends to operate.

Don't Come In craps, a bet placed after the come-out roll. Depending on the next roll, either: (1) two or three wins, (2) a twelve is a stand-off or, (3) seven or eleven loses.

Don't Pass Line In craps, the zone in which a player makes a don't pass bet.

Doorman The casino employee who admits players to the gaming room; more common in Europe.

Double Apron A cheating technique used by casino employees in which their normally pocketless apron is modified to create a pocket in which chips can be hidden.

Double Deal The process of dealing two cards together while pretending to deal only one.

Double Deck In blackjack, when two handheld decks are used.

Double Deuce Altered dice that have two deuces (the number two). The extra deuce takes the place of a five on the die.

Double Discard A draw poker cheating ploy whereby the hustler actually discards twice.

Double Down In blackjack, an option that allows the player to double the value of his wager after looking at the first two cards.

Double Duke A cheating technique used by a dealer who deals her victim a good hand but deals herself a better one.

33

Double Entry Bookkeeping   A system for recording financial transactions in which every transaction creates entries that affect at least two accounts.

Double Exposure   A variation of blackjack in which both the dealer's cards are shown before bettors play their hands; may have rule changes to compensate for this advantage being given to the bettors.

Double Number Dice   Dice that are misspotted so that one number appears twice on opposite sides of the die while another number is left off entirely.

Double Odds   In craps games at some casinos, when a player takes an odds bet at double the original stake.

Double Steer   A brief con in which the victim is led to believe he is going to be partners with a cheat in swindling a card or dice game.

Double the Bank   The goal of most card counters or teams to double the original playing stake.

Double Up   To enlarge a wager by an equal quantity.

Double Zero   Today, only American roulette wheels have two zeros, which is the thirty-eighth number on the wheel and green in color. (The first casino roulette wheel had two zeros.)

Doubling Up   To double the size of the preceding wager; serves as the basis for many betting strategies.

Down Behind   A losing don't come bet on a crap game. This call by the baseman alerts the boxman that they are removing the bet.

Drag Down   To retrieve all or part of a wager just won, thus not letting it ride on the next bet.

Dragging   Illegally removing chips from a wager after the game is in progress.

Dram Shop Legislation   Includes laws and procedures that govern the legal operation of establishments that sell measured alcoholic beverages.

Draw   (1) To take additional cards after the initial deal. (2) A form of poker.

Draw Ticket   A keno ticket that is punched by keno employees to reflect the numbers selected in the ball draw and used to verify winning tickets.

Driller   A cheating technique at the slot machines in which a hole is drilled in the machine to modify its play.

Drivers Seat   In stud poker, to have the best hand showing or to have won most of the money in a game.

Drop   During a given time frame, total amount of cash plus markers at a table, on a shift, or in an entire casino.

Drop Box   Box locked to the underside of a gaming table where the dealer deposits all currency, markers, and drop slips.

Drop Box Slot   An aperture in the table directly above the drop box, which includes the cover, or plunger, that allows items to be placed in the drop box.

Drop Bucket   A container that is stored in a locked cabinet in the base of the slot machine into which coins are diverted.

Drop Cabinet   A locked area usually found underneath each slot machine where the drop buckets are stored until the hard count team removes them during the slot drop process.

Drop Cut   A method of holding a stack of chips in one hand, touching them to the table and then lifting them, leaving a small stack of the correct number of chips. Also called *cut cheques* or *thumb cut.*

Dropping   The act during which the casino employee puts chips in the toke box.

Drown   To lose heavily.

Drunker Mitt   A short con game built around a poker game in which the con man 'accidentally' exposes his hand showing that he cannot win.

Dry   To lose all money or be broke, can refer to a single individual or many.

Due Diligence   (1) In legal terms, the pretrial activities to make every effort to obtain relevant facts to make the case. (2) A bundle of activities is a means to investigate or procure factual information garnered outside of the activities attendant on the formation, management, and enforcement of a contract for casino credit.

Duke   A big hand at a table.

Duking In   Involving a victim in a game by getting her to play for you or by making a bet for her.

Dummy Up and Deal   Old-time Nevada phrase used by a boss to tell a dealer to stop talking and speed up the game.

Dumping   To lose a great deal of money swiftly.

Dumping off a Game   A cheating technique in which a dealer allows her accomplice to win money from the casino.

Dump Shot   A sleight of hand technique for controlling the number on one of several dice rolled from a cup.

Dust Him Off   To flatter a player by suggesting that he is very smart.

E

EAP   An abbreviation for *Employee Assistance Program.*

Ear   A cheating technique in which a corner is bent on a playing card to identify or locate it.

Early Bird Ticket   A ticket to a bingo game sold at a special discount to induce players to come early.

Early Out   Term used by dealers when they get the last break before the end of the shift and, thus, can go home early.

Early Surrender   In blackjack, the player's option of relinquishing half the bet prior to the dealer determining if she has blackjack.

Earn   In casinos, the actual money the casinos can technically consider its take or revenue.

Earnest Money   The money required of the victim in certain con games as a show of good faith.

Earring   A cheating technique used by dealers in which they do not drop the paper money all the way into the drop box leaving one corner of the bill(s) exposed with the goal of retrieving it later; also called *hanger.*

Ease of Entry   Occurs for businesses when there are low capital requirements and no, or relatively low, licensing provisions thus making it easier to begin a business.

Easy Way   In craps, point made without paired numbers (e.g., making an eight with a five and a three rather than with 2 fours, which is the hard way).

Econometric Models   Statistical methods of analyzing data and making predictions about the future.

Economic Development   An economics term referring to the process by which less developed areas or regions increase their per capita output by improving their stock of capital goods such as building a casino or improving worker's skills, or by other means.

Economic Impact   An examination of the organization's effect on the external environments.

Ecotourism   Responsible travel to natural areas that conserves the environment and sustains the well being of the local people.

Edge   The mathematical advantage; usually retained by the house.

Edge Work (Edge Markings)   A cheating technique in cards in which they are marked with a slight bevel or belly drawn on a certain point of each card between the design and the edge of the card.

EEO   An abbreviation for *equal employment opportunity.*

EEOC   An abbreviation for *Equal Employment Opportunity Commission.*

Ego Strengths   A personality characteristic that measures the potency of a person's convictions.

Eighter from Decatur   In craps, the point eight.

Eighty-Six   (1) Used in casinos and restaurants to eject, evict, or try to get rid of a customer(s). (2) To close down a table, pit, or entire casino for the night.

Eighty-Sixed (86'ed)   A restaurant expression meaning an item is canceled or no longer available.

80-20 Principle   Eighty percent of the effort or resources is put into capturing twenty percent of the total sales volume.

Eldest Hand   The card player on the dealer's left.

Electric Dice   A cheating technique in craps in which the dice are loaded with steel slugs and used over an electric magnet hidden in or under a counter or dice table.

Element of Ruin   The probability that a player will lose their bank.

Elevator   A method of performing the hop in which the two halves of the deck are transposed by the right hand as it places the deck into the left hand to start the deal.

E-Mail   An abbreviation for electronic mail; a technology that allows individuals to send and receive reports over computer networks.

Employee   Nonmanagerial workers of an organization who perform tasks and are responsible only for their own actions.

Employee Assistance Program (EAP)   In companies, when counseling and other help is provided to workers having emotional, physical, or other personal problems.

Employee Burnout   Employees that do too much or have too much stress and become incapable of functioning effectively.

Empowerment   In business, increasing the decision-making discretion of workers.

Encoding   A psychological term referring to the process in which information from short-term memory is entered into long-term memory.

End of Day An arbitrary stopping point for the business day; established so that the audit can be considered complete through that time frame and is often at an hour other than midnight.

Enforcement The ability to compel a person to abide by the rules.

English (1) The simultaneous sliding and spinning action of the dice that is characteristic of most controlled shots. (2) Unique body movement, as in "body English."

English "American" Roulette A combination form of American roulette begun with the British Gaming Act of 1968, in which the double zero from the American type is eliminated, player differentiated chips are used, a single zero is derived from the French version, and the share half concession is used when zero appears.

En Plein In roulette, the French term for a wager on a single number.

En Prison French term used in roulette that permits the player to let her wager ride or surrender only half of it if a zero or double zero shows up.

Entrepreneurship A business term that refers to a process through which new business is created that involves uncertainty, risk, creative opportunism, and orientation toward growth.

Entropy The tendency of an organization to deteriorate.

Environmental Scanning In management, a method of identifying emerging environmental opportunities and threats that may influence the organization's performance.

Equal Employment Opportunity (EEO) In management, an employment-related decision must not be made based on factors such as race, color, religion, sex, national origin, or handicapped status.

Equal Employment Opportunity Commission (EEOC) Federal government agency created to administer the provisions of the Civil Rights Act of 1964, which contains laws regulating the staffing of organizations.

Equitable A fair game.

Equity Capital Funds supplied by the owner(s) of a business in return for the opportunity to share in the risks and rewards of the business.

ER Man Person who sits to the *extreme right* of the dealer; the *anchor*.

European Plan In hotels, a billing arrangement under which meals are priced separately from rooms.

Even Chances (Even Money) Odds of one to one.

Evening Shift Time frame for working that usually covers from 3 p.m. to 11 p.m.

Even Splitters   Dice which are so misspotted as to make it possible for the shooter to roll any of the even point numbers 4, 6, 8, 10.

Even Up   A wager made on even odds.

Exact Count   Equal to the running count divided by the conversion factor to indicate what the count would be if the game were being dealt from a single deck. Thus, if the running count is twelve, and three decks remain to be played, the exact count is twelve divided by three thus equaling four, indicating to the player that there is a relative surplus of two tens per fifty-two cards left to be played.

Executive Summary   A few pages usually positioned at the beginning of a marketing plan that sum up the plan's main sections.

Exit   To get out of the game.

Expectancy Theory   In management, a theory of motivation based on probability and the relationships among efforts, performance, and rewards.

Expected Value   The money the player should win or lose given average luck or in accordance with the statistical advantage of the casino. The *expected value* equals the player's advantage in percent multiplied by the total action.

Experimental Bias   A situation that occurs when an experimenter unintentionally communicates his own expectations onto the participants being studied. This behavior, although not intended to be part of the experimental manipulation, influences the participants.

Exposition   Event held mainly for information exchanges among trades people; large exhibition in which the presentation is the main attraction as well as a source of revenue for an exhibitor.

External Audit   Review of a firm's finances done by a public accounting firm.

External Environmental Forces   Factors outside the organization's control, including suppliers, customers, government, and unions that may affect performance and decision making.

Externalities   An activity that affects others, for better or worse, without those others paying or being paid for the activity, as in crime being suggested as a negative externality of casino gaming.

External Validity   The extent to which the research findings can be generalized to larger populations and applied to different settings.

Extreme Right Man (ER Man)   The player who sits at the dealer's extreme right at the blackjack table. He is the last to act on his hand before the dealer.

Extrinsic Rewards   Management term referring to rewards such as pay, promotion, praise, and benefits that an employee receives from others.

Eye (Eye in the Sky)   Electronic surveillance equipment suspended from the ceiling and tied into a central observation point.

F

F&B   An abbreviation for *food and beverage.*

Face Card   Jack, queen, or king.

Face Down   Method of delivering cards so that only the player sees them.

Face Validity   The investigator's subjective evaluation as to the validity of a measuring instrument; concerns the extent to which the measuring instrument appears to measure according to the researcher's subject assessment.

Factor Analysis   A statistical technique for classifying a larger number of interrelated variables into a smaller number of dimensions or factors.

Fad   A short-lived fashion or trend.

Fade (Fade Craps)   To cover all or part of the dice shooter's center bet.

Fade Cover   In craps or chemin de fer, a bet against the bank.

Fading Game   Open craps.

Fairbank   To make a cheating move in favor of the player to entice him to continue to play or to increase the size of his bet.

Fair Game   A game in which the payoffs are equal to the mathematical chances of winning. Casino games are not fair because the casino's payoffs are somewhat less than the mathematical probability of each result, and this small advantage will prove decisive over a long series of trials.

Faites Vos Jeux   French for "place your bets"; signals the start of betting at the roulette table.

False Carding   In draw poker, bluffing by taking fewer cards than is necessary to improve one's hand so that a position of strength is implied.

False Cut   A cut that leaves the deck, or part of the deck, in its original position.

Familiarization (Fam) Trips   Free or reduced priced trips given to travel agencies, tour wholesalers and operators, travel writers, and other intermediaries by suppliers, carriers, and destination marketing organizations.

Fan   To lay the deck of cards out on the table in a semicircular pattern for observation and verification.

Fan Tan   Simple oriental game played with beans or buttons in which the outcome is decided by a dealer dividing a pile of buttons with a stick, separating four at a time until four, then three, then one is left; found in some Nevada casinos.

FAQ   An abbreviation for *frequently asked question.*

Faro   Card game using a bank in which cards selected from the deck win sequentially or alternately for the bank and the players.

Fast Company   Sophisticated players who are capable of spotting the more crude methods of cheating and are more difficult to swindle.

Fast Count   (1) A rapid counting for the purpose of concealing a miscount of one or more numbers. (2) Shortchanging a person.

Fast Work   Playing cards that have been boldly marked so that they may be read more easily and quickly.

Fat   Person who has a large quantity of money; is loaded.

Favorites   Numbers or chances coming up frequently during certain times of a particular game.

Fax   An abbreviation for electronic facsimile.

Feasibility Analysis   A study of the potential demand and economic feasibility of a business or other type of organization.

Fever   (1) Gambling habit. (2) In craps, the number five.

Field   In craps, a wager good only for the next roll.

Field Splitters   A pair of misspotted dice, one of which bears only the numbers 1, 2, and 3 while the other bears only the numbers 4, 5, and 6.

FIFO (First In, First Out)   The supplies that are ordered first are used first.

Fill   Bringing additional checks from the cage to the table to replenish the dealer's bankroll.

Fill Slip   Voucher that goes along with the fill, is verified, and signed with one copy deposited in the drop box and one copy given to the floorperson by the dealer.

Fin   Five-dollar bill.

Finals   In roulette, the rightmost digits of the numbers on the wheel.

Finger   To identify a cheat.

Firm   (1) To hold or maintain one's wager. (2) Business unit.

First Base   In blackjack, the first seat or position immediately to the dealer's left and the player who receives the first card dealt.

First Basing   A cheating technique in blackjack in which the player in the first seat reads the dealer's hole card when it is picked up to see if he has a natural.

First Flop Dice   Loaded dice that have been so heavily weighted that they are likely to come up on the favored number on the first roll.

Five Card Charlie   A bonus popular in blackjack in which a five-card total equal to or less than twenty-one pays the player two to one.

Fix   To influence the outcome of a sports event or game to win a wager.

Fixed Cost   Financial liabilities that remain static or that do not vary with changes in business volume.

Flag   A die that has been modified so that it is not true.

Flagged   In craps, to be passed by as the next shooter.

Flash   To display a card, usually the dealer's hole card.

Flashing   A cheating technique in blackjack where the dealer exposes the top card of the deck to an accomplice to help her win.

Flash Work   A cheating technique in cards in which the entire back of each card, except for one small portion, is shaded lightly.

Flat Bet   To bet the same amount on each hand played.

Flat Joint (Flat Store)   Any crooked gambling game.

Flat Organization   Internal structure of a business in which a large number of subordinates report to one supervisor; characteristic of a new or small business.

Flat Passers   Crooked dice that have the 6 and 1 sides cut down on one die and the 3 and 4 sides cut down on the other so that 4, 5, 9, 10 appear more often.

Flats   Crooked dice that have been shaved so that two sides have more surface area than the other four sides; also called *bricks*.

Flea   (1) A patron who tries to ride on the winning of an ardent gambler or one who loiters in the casino attempting to obtain comps or other privileges. (2) Derogatory term used by casino employees for a small bettor.

Flick   A small hidden mirror that allows the cheat to see the faces of the cards as she deals them.

Float   In a table game, the tray.

Float Cover   The lid of the chip tray, which locks.

Floater   In roulette, when the ball hangs up under the lip and will not drop.

Floating Game   An illegal gambling game that is moved from place to place to avoid police raids.

Floats   Dice that are not true because they have been hollowed out and, thus, are so light that they seem to float.

Floorman (Floor Person)   Supervisor of the gaming tables who is responsible for keeping the racks full, attending to any problems at the tables, supervising the dealers, and watching for irregularities.

Floor Plan   The most common and informative type of blueprint that takes a straight down or bird's-eye perspective, often showing things like the position of gaming tables, cashiers, dining tables, and so on; sometimes referred to as a plan view.

Flopping the Deck   A cheating technique in blackjack in which the dealer secretly turns the deck over so the used, faceup cards on the bottom are dealt again.

Flush   (1) Gambler who is winning or has a lot of money. (2) In poker, a hand containing any five cards of one suit.

Flush Spotted Dice   Dice whose spots are flush with the surface rather than countersunk.

Focus Group   A form of personal interviewing in which the researcher asks open-ended questions to a small group of people to explore a topic.

Fold (Folding)   Throwing in a hand of cards or dropping out.

Folding Money   Paper money.

Folio (Guest Folio)   In hotels, a collection of guest charges that are recorded either manually or by a computer.

Food Cost Percentage   A ratio comparing the cost of food sold to food sales; calculated by dividing the cost of food sold during a given period by food sales during the same period.

Forecasting   Process of estimating future events in business.

Foreign Checks   Cheques that are received from another casino.

Foreign Chips   Chips from another casino.

Formal Communications Channels   In an organization, those communication flows that follow the formal organizational relationships depicted by an organization chart.

Fortified Wines   Wine to which brandy or other spirits have been added to stop any further fermentation and/or to raise its alcoholic strength.

Four-Eyed   Term used to describe a cheat who specializes in the use of a glim (a cheating move to see cards as they are being dealt).

Four of a Kind   In poker, all four cards are the same rank.

Four-Way-Play Bingo   A game in which there are four winning positions; also called *round robin*.

Franchising   A contractual arrangement between a franchisor (who owns the name and style of operation) and a franchisee that allows the franchisee to conduct business under an established name and according to a given pattern of business in return for a fee. Widely used in hotels and chain restaurants.

Free Bet   In bank craps, a bet that permits a player who has made a previous bet on the pass or don't pass line to lay or take the correct point odds equal to the amount she is playing on the line.

Free Double Odds Bet   Same as free bet except that right or wrong bettors with line bets can take or lay double the amount riding on the line.

Free Hand   The hand in which the shoe is not normally held while dealing.

Free Ride   Playing part of a poker hand without betting; a losing bet that goes unnoticed and plays again.

Freeze Out   To force a gambler out of a game.

French Service   Restaurant service in which one waiter (a captain) takes the order, does the tableside cooking, and brings the drinks and food. A secondary or back waiter serves bread and water, clears each course, crumbs the table, and serves the coffee.

French Wheel   European roulette wheel that contains only one zero located between black twenty-six and red thirty-two.

Frequency Distribution   The number of observations of each value of a variable.

Frets   In roulette, the dividers that create the pockets on the wheel.

Front Desk   In lodging, the focal point of activity within the front office where the guest checks in, is assigned a room, and checks out; usually located in the lobby.

Front Line   In craps, the pass line.

Front Line Odds   Taking the odds on the point number.

Front Loader   In blackjack, a careless dealer who uncovers her hole card while dealing.

Front Man   A person who does not have a criminal record who poses as the owner of a casino when he really is not; done in an effort to circumvent the law.

Front Money   Funds put forth by a player to establish credit in a casino.

Front of the House   The functional areas of the casino, hotel, or restaurant in which employees have extensive guest contact such as the casino floor, front desk, or dining room.

Fruit Machine   Term used by the English for a slot machine because the earliest slot reels used fruit as symbols.

Full House   In poker, a hand with three of a kind plus a pair.

Full Moon   Term used by dealers to refer to the time of the month when (they think) all the strange people or "turkeys" come to their table.

Full-Service Hotel   Hotel that has restaurants, lounges, concierges, and many more facilities to cater to guests' needs.

Full-Service Restaurant   A restaurant that has more than a dozen or so main course items on the menu, cooks food to order, and uses cloth napery.

Full Table   A crowded craps table.

Functional Authority   In management, the authority to make decisions and prescribe policies, procedures, and other matters for a specialized area of operations such as accounting, finance, and so on.

Furniture Man   A cheat who specializes in switching cards by means of a holdout machine.

G

G (Gaff or Gimmick)   Any secret cheating device.

Galloping Dominoes   Pair of dice.

Gambler's Fallacy   The erroneous belief that because an event has not occurred recently in a series of independent trials, it becomes more likely to occur in the future as in staying at a single slot machine or betting a certain number.

Gambler's Ruin   The risk that a gambler will run out of money or lose his entire bankroll.

Gambling   To make a prediction of an uncertain outcome and then back the decision with money.

Game Bankroll   Refers to the house's gaming cheques maintained on the table; increases or decreases to the bankroll are accomplished through fill or credit transactions and through player transactions. Also known as *table float* or *inventory*.

45

Games   Casino gaming activities that use dealers and do not include slot machines.

Gaming Board (Commission)   In some jurisdictions, the name of the government appointed authority that regulates casino gaming.

Gate   In craps, when officials or employees of the casino stop the dice before they have finished rolling because they fear foul play.

George   (1) Player who plays very well. (2) Player who gives the dealer cash. (3) Player who makes bets on behalf of the dealer.

Get Behind the Stick   In craps, when a stickman or dealer goes to work or opens the game.

Gets the Money   Any cheating technique that is highly effective in winning the other players' money.

GGR   An abbreviation for *gross gaming revenue.*

G.I. Marbles   Dice.

Gimmick   Something used to fix or alter a game.

Give Him the Bum's Rush   To eject a player without dignity.

Give the Business   (1) To cheat someone. (2) To ignore someone.

Glass House   A management term referring to the situation in which everyone views all decisions and actions.

Glim   A cheating technique, which employs a small hidden mirror, that allows the cheat to see the faces of the cards as they are dealt.

Glim Worker   A card cheat who uses a small hidden mirror that allows him to see the faces of the cards as they are being dealt.

GM   An abbreviation for *general manager.*

G-Note   One-thousand dollar bill.

Go   Term used by dealers when talking about the amount of tips made, as in "What did you go yesterday?"

Go for the Money   To cheat.

Good Man   (1) A player with much money. (2) Someone who is an adept cheater.

Good Thing   A sound wager.

Goose   In keno, the tube where balls collect after being forced through an air stream.

Go Over   In blackjack, when anyone exceeds twenty-one; also called *break* or *bust.*

Gorilla   A noncounting player who receives signals from a counter.

Go South With   To secretly palm cards, dice, money, or anything else and take it out of action.

Goulash   Any business establishment such as a bar or restaurant that conducts card games on a regular basis in the back room.

Grand   One thousand dollars.

Grapevine   In an organization, the informal, lateral communications through which a few individuals relate information to others.

Graveyard Shift   The last work shift, usually lasting until early morning.

Gravity Model   A site-selection method based on the premise that people frequent businesses that are closer and more attractive than competitors'.

Greek Deal   A cheating technique in which the second card from the bottom of the deck is dealt while pretending to deal off the top.

Greek Shot   In craps, a controlled throw of the dice.

Green   (1) Cash. (2) Twenty-five dollar chips that are green in color.

Green Horn   An inexperienced gambler.

Green Numbers   In roulette, the zero and double zero.

Grief   Bad luck or difficulty.

Grievance Procedure   A formal channel of communication, often found in companies with unions; used to resolve job-related complaints.

Griffin Agent   An employee of the most renowned Griffin Detective Agency who is hired by numerous casinos to detect slot and gaming cheats, dishonest employees, and card counters.

Grift   All categories of theft in which the victim is robbed through trickery rather than force.

Grifter   A dishonest gambler.

Grind Houses (Joint)   Casinos catering to low-end players (low rollers) but requiring high volume of play.

Gross Gaming Revenue   The net spending of customers on gaming, not including spending on nongaming operations such as food and beverage, hotel rooms, and other retail expenditures.

Gross Operating Profit   Revenues minus operating costs before taxes.

Gross Revenues   In accounting, total incoming sales; specific to casinos, refers to the net win resulting from deducting all gaming losses from all wins prior to considering associated operating expenses; also known as *gross gaming revenue* and *win*.

Group Norms   Unwritten rules of conduct established to maintain consistent and desired behavior within the group; often found in business.

Group I Licensee   In Nevada, a nonrestricted casino licensee that either (1) has annual gross gaming revenue of $4 million or more, or (2) consists primarily of a race or sports pool that accepts annual wagers of $50 million or more.

Group II Licensee   In Nevada, a nonrestricted casino licensee that either (1) has annual gross gaming revenue of more than $1 million, but less than $3 million, or (2) consists primarily of a race or sports pool that accepts annual wagers of more than $10 million, but less than $50 million.

Guaranteed Reservations   If hotel rooms are available when a guest makes a reservation then the hotel guarantees the guest rooms on those days and the guest assumes payment, usually using a credit card.

H

Hand   (1) In a card game like blackjack, the player's cards. (2) In craps, the total length of time and number of rolls for one shooter from the come-out roll.

Handicapper   Track official who assigns weights to certain horses in a race.

Handicap Room   In lodging, a guest room with special features designed to meet the needs of handicapped guests.

Handle   Total amount of money that continually changes hands through a series of bets before it is actually won or lost.

Handle Slamming   A cheating technique at the slot machines in which the cheat tries to control the reel combination that comes up by first pulling the handle and then slamming it back upward.

Hand Mucker   A cheating move in cards in which the perpetrator palms or switches the cards he has been dealt.

Hand Off   A cheating technique in which the dealer secretly transfers chips to an associate who is posing as a player.

Hand Signal   When a player uses her hand to inform the dealer whether or not she wants another card.

Hanger   A cheating technique in which the dealer does not drop paper money all the way into the box, leaving a corner exposed with the expectation of retrieving it later; also called *earring*.

Hang the Flag   A signal from a casino cheat to his partners that no cheating should take place at the moment because of heavy surveillance.

Hard Count   The process of counting the coins and tokens removed from the slot machine drop buckets through the use of a weight scale or coin counter; performed by designated count personnel, also known as a *count team*, in a secured room that is monitored by surveillance cameras.

Hard-Count Room   The secured room used to weigh, wrap, record, and verify the contents of the slot drop buckets. The hard count room can also act as a storage facility for the casino cage.

Hard Hand (Hard Total)   In blackjack, a hand that does not include an ace, or in which an ace can only be valued as one if the total of the hand is not to exceed twenty-one.

Hard Opening   When a complete operation is totally functional at the hour of inauguration of the property.

Hard Rock   (1) In poker, a tight player. (2) A gambler who refuses to lend money. (3) A player who is difficult to beat.

Hard Way   In craps, the numbers four, six, eight, and ten made by having the dice come up as a pair (e.g., 2 fives to make ten rather than a six and a four).

Has a Sign on His Back   Gambler who is known on sight by the casinos and is regarded as a cheater.

Hawking the Dice   A base dealer on one end of the table looking at the roll of the dice on the opposite end. (This is not permitted.)

Hay   Money or chips.

Head   (1) In roulette, the part of the wheel that spins and fits into the bowl. (2) The restroom.

Head Count   Number of people.

Head On   When a player is alone at the table and is playing against the dealer.

Head to Head   Playing alone with the dealer as the only player at the table.

Heart   Courage, fortitude, or "guts."

Heat   (1) In blackjack, statements by casino employees that suggest to players that they are suspected of card counting. (2) Heavy surveillance that tends to reduce cheating. (3) Close scrutiny, pressure, or criticism of the dealer by bosses.

Heavy Hand   A hand of cards that, unbeknown to others, has more cards than it should have.

Heel   (1) A stingy gambler. (2) A jerk. (3) To separate a wager made with more than one color of chip. (4) To place one cheque of a marker on top of another cheque angled in the direction of the player.

Heel Peek   A method of secretly glimpsing at the top card of the deck by lifting the inner corner of the card with the base of the thumb; also used when dealing out of the shoe before exposing a card.

Heist   A deck of cards altered so that cards with high numerical values can be controlled.

Hierarchy   In management, the division of authority among levels of management.

Hierarchy of Effect Model   The sequence of steps a consumer goes through, in reacting to promotion, that leads them from awareness to knowledge to liking to preference to conviction to purchase.

High/Low   In craps, a split bet on two and twelve.

High-Low Pickup   A method of cheating at blackjack that involves picking up the discards in a high-low alternating order.

High-Low Splitters   A pair of misspotted dice that has only the numbers 1, 2, and 3, whereas the other has only the numbers 4, 5, and 6; used by the house to beat the player who bets on the field at craps.

High Roller (High Stakes Gambler)   A premium player; anyone able and willing to spend five-thousand dollars or more in a weekend of gambling. (There are an estimated 35,000 high rollers in the world.)

Hipster   Someone who has a good knowledge of odds and percentages, or of cheating and cheating devices.

Hit   In blackjack, to request another card from the dealer.

Hit and Run   To win quickly and then leave the game.

Hit It   To make the desired point or number.

Hits   Dice gaffed so as to favor the shooter.

Hit the Boards   (1) To leave or depart. (2) In craps, when the stickman asks the shooter to be sure to throw the dice against the rail.

Hitting Hand   A two-card hand with the value of eleven or less requiring an additional card or cards to complete the hand.

Hold   Proportion of player outlays retained by the house after redeeming chips and slot machine tokens.

Hold Check   A check received from a player as payment on a casino receivable and which the player requests are held for a specified period of time before it is deposited. The casino may return the marker to the player at this time, and the check will become the instrument supporting the receivable balance.

Holdout   A cheating technique in which cards are kept out of play with the plan of later switching them for cards that have been dealt.

Holdout Artist   A gambler or cheat who, when calculating the score or dividing the amount of winnings with her partner or partners, says that her winnings are less so she can pocket the difference.

Holdout Man   A card cheat who specializes in palming cards to take them out of play and then reintroduces valuable cards into a game by means of palming.

Holdout Shoe   A blackjack shoe that has been gaffed so as to allow the dealer to deal seconds whenever he wishes.

Holdout Table   A card table that has been elaborately gaffed so as to conceal a card until the cheat wishes to retrieve it.

Hold Percentage   The amount of money won by the casino expressed as a percentage of the amount of money or credit exchanged for gaming chips (the drop).

Hole Card   (1) A card dealt face down or concealed in blackjack or poker. (2) In blackjack, the dealer's bottom card usually dealt face down.

Hole Card Play   Any of a number of cheating techniques in blackjack in which the cheat tries to catch a glimpse of the dealer's hole card.

Hook   A half point in a bet on a sporting event that eliminates a tie, as in "I've got the Raiders by a hook."

Hooked   To lose money.

Hop   A cheating technique in which cards are brought back to their original order after being cut by another player.

Hop Bet   In craps, a one-roll bet that may be bet at any time on a specific combination of the dice. A hardway pays 31 to 1 and a two-way combination pays 15 to 1. These are placed in front of the boxperson.

Hopper   A device within the slot machine that holds a predetermined amount of coin used to pay out player winnings.

Hopper Fill Slip   A document that is used to record the replenishments of the coins in the hopper that is required as a result of payouts to players; indicates the amount of coin placed into the hoppers, as well as the signatures of the employees involved in the transaction, the machine number and location, and the date.

Horizon   In lodging, the future time frame for which a reservation is accepted.

Horizontal Integration   Having representation in the multiple sectors of the market place. May be achieved by purchasing or developing a midscale hotel chain or an all-suite or economy chain, so the corporation has representation in each price range.

Hospitality Operations   The management of the activities involved in producing the goods or services of an organization involved in sheltering, feeding, transporting, and entertaining people.

Host   Casino employee whose job it is to ensure that valued or rated players are satisfied with the casino and its services; also handles some marketing, promotions, invitations to special events, and so on.

Hot   (1) In craps, when dice rolls produce more passes than misses. (2) In a card game, when the deck or shoe is favorable to the player.

Hot Deck   A deck or shoe favorable to the player.

Hot Number   A number that has a better chance of being hit than any other number.

Hot Player   A player on a winning streak.

Hot Score   The profits of a gambling scam when accompanied by an argument from the victim.

Hot Seat Game   A card game in which every player is part of the cheating group except for one unsuspecting victim.

House   Casino, casino employees, casino's funds or bank.

House Advantage (Percentage)   Mathematical winning edge that the casino gives itself by manipulating the rules of the games to ensure profitability.

House Dealer   Dealer who is winning.

House Limit   A credit limit established by the casino or hotel.

House Numbers   In roulette, the zero and double zero which, when they come up, allow a profit for the casino in all even money bets.

HRIS   An abbreviation for *human resources information system.*

Hub   (1) In computers, a central location for processing before the information is dispersed. (2) In transportation, a central terminal from which all transportation leaves and returns.

Human Capital   The stock of technical skill and knowledge embodied in a region's work force, resulting from formal education and on-the-job training.

Human Resources   The department that focuses on the people in the organization.

Human Resources Information System (HRIS)   An integrated, computerized system designed to provide information to be used in making personnel decisions.

Hunch Player   A gambler who bets impulsively with little knowledge of the game.

Hustler   A person who cheats at gambling.

Hustling   Actions that induce a gift or a tip.

Hypothesis   A tentative answer to a research problem expressed in the form of a relation between independent and dependent variables.

Hypster   A cheater who specializes in shortchanging cashiers.

I

Ice   Protection money.

Iceman   Bagman; person who collects money.

IGRA   An abbreviation for *Indian Gaming Regulatory Act.*

IGT   An abbreviation for *International Gaming Technologies, Inc.*

Image   How a business is viewed, either positively or negatively, by consumers.

Impair   In roulette, wagering that the winning number will be odd.

In   Quantity of money that a player has traded for chips at the table; also called a *buy-in.*

In Balance   An accounting term used to describe the state when the totals of debit amounts and credit amounts are equal.

Incentives   In management, rewards designed to encourage and reimburse employees for efforts beyond normal performance expectations.

Incentive Travel   Travel by persons who have received travel packages as a reward for outstanding performance.

Incentive Travel Planners   Specialized tour wholesalers who assemble incentive packages for sponsoring organizations.

Income   The flow of wages, interest, dividends, and other receipts accruing to an individual, firm, or region.

Income Statement   Financial document that encapsulates the performance of an organization for a specified period of time.

Independent Agent   An individual located outside the casino location (usually a different city) and not employed by the casino who attracts customers who wish to play in the casino; compensated with a commission based on head count or the customers' play.

Independent Variable   Variable hypothesized to explain variations in the dependent variable.

Index   The numbers in the upper left and lower right of a player card that indicate its value.

Indian Dice   A traditional Native American bar game using five dice and allowed under Class I gaming; each player gets three throws with the object to build the best possible poker hand; there are no straights and a one is wild.

Indian Gaming   A term referring to the betting on uncertain outcomes on Native American reservations.

Indian Gaming Regulatory Act (IGRA)   A 1988 federal regulation, which established rules and three levels for Native American gambling. (See Class I, Class II, and Class III Gaming.)

Indicator   On the big six wheel, the clapper that indicates the winning space.

Industry   Group of firms or businesses producing similar goods or services.

Inflation   The increase in volume of money and credit, resulting in the continuing rise of the general price level.

Information Overload   Too much information; generally referring to a tendency of information systems and their users to generate and send too much or nonuseful information to guests and employees.

Initial Fill   A predetermined amount of coins that are placed into the hopper when a new slot machine is placed on the casino floor; the beginning inventory of coins for each slot machine; recorded as "other assets" on the books of the casino and are not deductible expenses.

Innovation   In business, the creation or acquisition of new technology.

Innovator   (1) In management, a person who is creative and approaches problems from a new perspective. (2) In marketing, a person who tries new products first.

In Prison (en prison)   In European roulette, when the ball lands on zero, even money bets are offered two choices: partage and *in prison*. If the gambler selects *in prison*, depending on the next spin, the player can recover but without a payoff, or he loses.

Inputs   Raw data that are entered in the information system.

Inside   The casino's position in the games.

Inside Man   Casino employee who handles the books or finances.

Inside Straight   In poker, a sequence of cards that needs an internal or middle card to complete the sequence.

Inside Ticket   The keno ticket that is presented by the player with her selections and amount wagered indicated; the ticket is retained by the casino.

Inside Work   Any gaffs.

Instrumental Conditioning   A learning theory that views behavior as a reaction to a stimulus because of expected reinforcement. (For example, Sally sees a slot machine at the end of the aisle, pulls the lever, and receives ten dollars. The next time this situation occurs, Sally will likely try again because she was rewarded with ten dollars the last time.)

Insurance   In blackjack, a wager that the dealer has a ten-card face down when an ace is showing; pays two to one.

Insurance Counter   A player who uses a special count, perfect for the insurance bet. He often signals the correct insurance play to another counter, who is playing a different system.

Insurance Line   In blackjack, the place on the table where the insurance bet is placed.

Interdependency   When changes in one part of the organization affect all other parts of the organization.

Intermodal Transportation   Using a combination of transportation modes to take advantage of the benefits of each during its portion of the transportation task, as in using planes then buses to transport people to a casino.

Internal Audit   Financial review performed by company personnel.

Internal Customer   Persons or units within the organization that depend on and serve each other.

Internal Environment   Tangible and intangible factors that exist within the organization and are under its control.

Internal Organizational Forces   Factors inside the organization including personnel, organization structure, policies, resources, and relationships that may affect managerial decision making.

In the Chips   Having a lot of money.

In the Clear   Free of debt.

In the Red   (1) In debt. (2) Losing.

Intrinsic Rewards   Rewards that originate with the person due to satisfaction with the work itself, achievements, and self-esteem.

J

Jackpot   Largest payout from a slot machine.

Jackpot Light-Up Board   An electric sign that hangs in a slot machine parlor or gambling establishment and is connected to the slot machines; lights up and a chime rings when a jackpot is hit.

Jackpot Payout Refers to a jackpot, or a portion of a jackpot, that is paid to the player directly by slot employees instead of from the machine hopper; also known as a *hand pay*.

Jackpot Payout Slip A document that is used to record the amount of a jackpot paid to the player by slot employees; includes the signatures of the employees involved in the transaction, the amount paid to the player, the machine number and location, the winning combination, and the date.

Jai Alai A game similar to squash or handball and played by two or more persons involving a ball (pelota) and a device called a *cesta*, which is made from wicker and is used to receive and hurl the pelota again the wall.

Jeton French chip or token.

Jimbroni A slow-thinking dealer.

Jit Five cents.

Job Description An outline of the basic tasks, duties, and responsibilities of a particular work assignment.

Job Shadowing A person working in a certain field, but also training for another.

Job Specification The qualifications such as knowledge, skills, and abilities required of a person to perform a work assignment satisfactorily.

Jog A cheating technique in which a card protrudes slightly from the deck to act as a marker; used during illegal shuffles and cuts.

Johnson Act Federal legislation passed in the 1950's that abolished any use of slot machines.

Joint A casino.

Joint Bank Situation in which two players combine their resources and play together off the total sum, sharing in the win or loss.

Joint Venture A partnership between an organization and host firm, or firms, to finance and manage a cooperatively owned enterprise; often found in Native American casinos.

Joker An extra card furnished with each fifty-two-card deck and occasionally used as a wild card to represent any card.

Jug Jail.

Juice (1) Power, influence, knowing the right people. (2) In baccarat, the vigorish. (3) Electricity. (4) Influence in getting things accomplished. (5) Bookmaker's commission.

Juice Deck   Cards that have been marked by a method that makes the markings literally invisible to anyone who has not been taught how to see them; a cheat can easily read the marks from up to ten feet away.

Juice Joint   A cheating technique in which the roulette wheel or dice game is electronically controlled.

Junior Jackpot Ticket Bingo   Tickets that pay off a smaller jackpot.

Junket   A form of comp in which a group of known and rated gamblers are brought to the casino on an all-inclusive trip paid for by the casino and are expected to participate in a given level of casino action.

Junket Representative   Individual who is responsible for organizing junkets; may be an employee of the casino or an independent agent.

K

Keno   A lottery type of casino game that is often played off the casino floor in which players win by picking up to twenty numbers, which are subsequently drawn from among eighty numbers; one number pays two to one on three to one odds, thus giving the casino a 25 percent edge; the more numbers the players choose commensurately, the greater the odds.

Keno Runner   Employee who sells keno tickets and delivers winning payoffs to customers outside the keno area.

Key Employee   An executive, employee, or agent of a casino licensee who may have a significant influence on the gaming operation.

Kibitzer   Spectator who often makes unsolicited and unwanted comments to the players.

Kick Back   (1) To return part or all of a score to a mark to avoid a beef. (2) To return a percentage of a player's losses as a marketing tool to secure future business.

Kill (a Number)   To control a die during a roll so that a desired number comes up.

King Kong   In dealer's jargon, a player who bets a lot for the dealer.

Kitty   A pool of money (either all or part) that goes to the winner of a hand or round of wagering.

Knock (a Mark)   For an outsider to convince the potential victim of a gambling scam or con game that he is being swindled.

Knock Out   A cheating term in a casino referring to when a dealer takes all the money from a player, as in "I *knocked out* the guy from New York."

L

Labor Cost Percentage   Similar to food cost percentage, except it relates to labor; the formula is labor costs divided by net sales multiplied by 100.

Labor Force (or Supply)   The availability of trained and willing workers in a region to fill organizational positions.

Labor Intensive   Relying on a large work force to meet the needs of guests.

Lace   In baccarat, a technique for mixing the cards after the shuffle.

Ladder Man   Casino employee who sits on a high stool or platform to oversee and supervise the game.

Lammer   (1) Small disc used to show the value of a chip or check. (2) Signify the use of credit. (3) Someone who is running away, usually from the law.

Lammer Button   Similar in appearance to a chip; placed on the table to indicate the amount of chips given on credit to a player for wagering purposes prior to the completion of a marker; also referred to as a *marker button*.

LAN   An abbreviation, in computers, for a *local area network* of computers.

Land-Based Casino   A casino that is totally constructed and physically supported on the land, rather than on water.

Larceny   The inclination to take advantage of a dishonest opportunity when it comes along.

Las Vegas Strip   The street in Las Vegas named Las Vegas Boulevard, the largest gaming area in Las Vegas, Nevada.

Late Bet   In roulette, placing a winning wager after the call has been made for no more bets.

Law of Demand   Theory that consumers usually purchase more units at a low price than at a high price.

Lay and Pay   Approach of turning over a player's cards or taking wagers followed by gathering all the used cards at once, as in "Most of the joints are *lay and pay*."

Lay Bet   In craps, a wager that seven will roll before the number wagered on; a house commission is charged on the true dice odds amount that could be won.

Lay Down   A bet or wager.

Layoff   A wager made by one race or sports book at another in order to reduce the amount of risk that results from having accepted too much in wagers on one side of a particular event.

Layout   (1) The felt covering of a table for games such as blackjack or roulette, which contains designations for the betting areas, usually in green, sometimes in red, rarely in blue, and imprinted in white. (2) Internal design.

Leader Pricing   A form of promotional pricing in which one or more services or products is offered for a short time at a price below its actual cost.

Leadership   In management, an activity that consists of influencing other people's behavior, individual and as a group, toward the achievement of desired objectives.

Leads   Prospective clients.

Leak   To fail to completely hide a cheating move such as allowing a palmed card to show between the cheat's fingers.

Lean Environment   A service setting, environment, or servicescape requiring that guests process relatively little information; used when guests are generally unfamiliar with the environment.

Legal Tie   (1) In blackjack, when a dealer's count is the same as the player's count. (2) In poker, when two players have the same ranking hand.

Legit Game   An honest game.

Le Grand   In baccarat, when two cards total nine.

Let It Ride   To replay a winning bet including the original bet and the winnings.

Levels   Any honest gaming equipment, particularly dice.

Leverage   Financial concept that compares the proportion of funds provided internally to those proved by external creditors.

Liabilities   Financial term that refers to debts owed by a firm.

Liberty Bell   The first slot machine invented in San Francisco in 1895 by Charles Fey, a twenty-nine year-old mechanic and the first slot machine operator in America.

Licensee   Any person to whom a valid gaming license is used.

Lid   The cover that is placed over the tray or rack on a table game and is locked.

Life Cycle   The useful life of a product in a given market that includes the stages of introduction, growth, maturity, and decline.

Lifestyles   The ways in which individual consumers and families or households live and spend time and money.

Light   (1) Any device that allows the cheat to observe the cards as she deals them; same as a glim. (2) Insufficient amount. (3) Weak.

Light Bet   A wager that is below the table minimum.

Light Work   Altered cards marked with very fine lines.

Limit   Maximum or minimum bet allowed.

Limited Stakes Gaming   A type of gaming in which the maximum bet is five dollars on any gaming device.

Limit Play   When either money or checks are being played to the posted table limit.

Line   Amount of credit a player has with the casino.

Linear Programming   Mathematical aid for decision makers who wish to maximize some desired objective or minimize some undesired result, subject to limitations.

Line Bet   (1) In roulette, a bet on six numbers in two rows of three numbers each running across the layout; the payoff is five to one odds. (2) In craps, same as the pass-line bet.

Line Bus   In casinos, the bus program in which the carriers charge a fare and organize it.

Line Work   On altered cards, additional small spots, curlicues, or lines added to the back design of the cards so that they can be read by the cheat.

Liquidity Ratios   Financial ratios that indicate the capability of an organization to pay its debts.

Live One   A player with money.

Load   In craps, a method of cheating in which weight is placed inside the dice to alter the characteristics.

Loader   Careless dealer who shows the hole card while dealing.

Location Play   Memorizing a group of cards in sequence so that when one of the cards appears during the game, the cheat will know that the valued ones are about to follow.

Locked Up   When a dealer has to work a game for longer than normal without a break.

Lock Up   To safely store money in the toke box or rack.

Locus of Control   An organizational theory term that refers to a personality attribute that measures the degree to which people believe they are masters of their own fate.

Long Bet   A wager that exceeds the table limit.

Long Green   Cash; paper money.

Looking for Action   A gambler looking for a game.

Lookout   A casino employee who acts as an observer of the floor or games to ensure smooth operation through surveillance.

Loose   (1) In slot machines, a unit with a high payback rate. (2) A person with low morals or one who is promiscuous.

Lottery   In gaming, a randomized drawing from a pool, usually of sold tickets.

Low Belly Strippers   A marked deck of cards in which the edges of the high cards are concave rather than straight, making it possible for the cheat to cut to a low or high card.

Low Roller   A person who makes one- and two-dollar bets; also known as *grinds, suckers,* or *tinhorns.*

Luck   (1) The inexplicable. (2) Anything not due to skill, statistics, or science.

Lugger   An individual who delivers gamblers to a game.

Luminous Readers   A cheating technique in cards in which a substance is placed on the backs of the cards that can only be seen through special tinted glasses.

M

Machiavellianism   A measure of the degree to which people are pragmatic, maintain emotional distance, and believe that ends justify means.

Machine (Holdout Machine)   A mechanical device worn on a cheater's chest that allows him to retain certain cards and keep them out of play until later.

Machine Fill   The transfer of coin or tokens from a slot booth or the casino cage to a slot machine whose hopper is low on coins.

Magnet   In cheating, a person who places a magnet on the side of older slot machines to get the inside wheels to obtain winning combinations and payouts and then pulls the magnet off when finished.

Mallard   A hundred-dollar bill.

Managed Services   Services that can be outsourced to professional management companies.

Management   The effective and efficient integration and coordination of resources in order to achieve desired objectives.

Management Contract   An agreement between the owner/developer of a facility and a professional management company in which the owner/developer usually retains the financial and legal responsibility for the facility while the management company receives an agreed upon fee and/or percentage for operating the facility.

Management Functions   The major activities of management including planning, organizing, directing, and controlling.

Management Information System (MIS)   An organized method of providing past, present, and projected information relating to internal and external operations to assist in decision making.

Manager   Person in an organization who undertakes management functions including planning, organizing, directing, and controlling and, thus, coordinates activities to guide the organization toward its desired goals.

Man Upstairs   (1) Casino employee's term for top management. (2) The casino employees who work in surveillance monitoring the cameras of the eye in the sky.

Mark   The target of a con man.

Marker   An IOU or credit extended to a player.

Marker Card   A card positioned in the deck or shoe to signify the end of play.

Marker Down   A communicative phrase to the floorperson indicating that the marker has been repaid.

Marker Puck   In craps, a large saucer-shaped object approximately three inches across; it is black on one side on which the word "OFF" is written and white on the side on which the word "ON" is written.

Marker System   Credit play system that allows the casino to both issue and redeem markers in the pit.

Marketing Mix   The combination of variables over which marketers have control; include price, product, place, and promotion.

Market Niche   Usually a small and specialized portion of a market, sometimes called a *segment*.

Market Segment   A group of people whose members have something in common and to which a specific service appeals.

Market Share (1) Percentage relationship of an organization's sales to total industry sales. (2) Fraction of an industry's output accounted for by an individual firm or group of firms.

Mark Off The process by which the dealer separates stacks of chips in the rack into the proper size so that a floorperson can quickly and accurately count them from a distance.

Martingale In roulette, a doubling up system of wagering.

Mason A stingy player.

Master Game Report A form, usually computer generated, that summarizes information for each table to determine the win or loss for the table; also known as a *stiff sheet*, indicates the amount of currency and chips removed from the drop box as well as fills, credits, and marker transactions that occurred at the table.

Match Up To locate or make a pair of gaffed dice that are identical in appearance to the dice in play.

Maximum The largest bets allowed per chance and per player, as set by the casino.

Mean (1) Nasty person. (2) In statistics, the same as average.

Mechanic A dealer who is very good at cheating and manipulating the cards.

Mechanical Games Games that require little or no skill, such as slot machines or pull-tabs.

Mechanic's Grip A method of holding a deck of cards, in either the left or right hand, with three fingers curled around the long edge of the deck and the index finger at the narrow upper edge away from the body.

Mechanistic Organization An organization that tends to be inflexible and, thus, resists change.

Median In mathematics, the figure in the exact middle of a series of numbers ordered or ranked from lowest to highest.

Mega-Resorts A self-contained, destination property that includes, at a minimum, hotel, restaurants, swimming pools, tennis courts, and other amenities.

Memphis Dominoes Dice.

Mentor A person who sponsors, supports, or guides another employee who is lower in the organization.

Meter A mechanical device contained in the slot machine, which may record information such as the number of coins placed into the machine, the number of coins paid out, and the number of coins dropped in the drop bucket. (Computerized slot systems also contain meters to record the same type of information.)

Mexican Standoff   A wagering session that ends in either incidental winnings or losses.

Michigan Bankroll   Wads of money in which a large denomination bill is wrapped around a core of one-dollar bills in an attempt to make the player appear to have more money.

Mini-Baccarat   A baccarat game played on a smaller, blackjack style table with one dealer who distributes all the cards, rather than passing the shoe from player to player; usually has lower minimum wagers than baccarat.

Minimum   The lowest wager allowed to be placed at a table.

Minus Count   A cumulative negative count of the cards placed in play that tends to be to the disadvantage of the player.

MIS   An abbreviation for *management information system.*

Miss a Pass   Failure to make a point number in craps.

Misses   Dice so gaffed as to work against the shooter.

Mission   The stated and basic written objective of the organization that serves to guide it; conveyed to others through the mission statement.

Missout   In craps, failure to make the point.

Misspots   Misspotted dice that have certain numbers repeated on opposite sides whereas other numbers have been left off entirely.

Mitt   A hand of cards.

Mitting In   To get a victim involved in playing in a game by getting him to play for the cheat or by making a bet for him.

Mitt Man   A card cheat who specializes in palming and switching the cards she has been dealt.

Mixed Stack   A pile of chips that contains several denominations or colors.

Mode   A measure of central tendency defined as the most frequently occurring observation category in the data.

Mode of Transportation   Transportation option that is chosen such as airplane, bus, boat, car, and so on.

Modified American Plan (MAP)   Packages that include accommodation and two meals per day (normally breakfast and dinner).

Moment of Truth   A term used to describe service encounters when a customer directly interacts with an employee.

Money Play   A call on any of the games to alert the floorperson that cash is being placed as a bet.

Money Poker   A guessing game played with dollar bills; also known as *liar poker*.

Money Switch   A dice switch performed under the cover of the bills that the cheat holds in her hand for betting.

Money Wheel   The big six wheel.

Monitor   Part of the surveillance system by which the output from the eye in the sky is displayed.

Monkey   (1) Face card. (2) A sucker.

Monopolistic Competition   In economics, a term referring to a market structure in which there is a large number of sellers who are supplying goods that are close, but not perfect, substitutes.

Morning Line   In horse and dog racing, the handicapper's or price-maker's morning guess as to the probable odds that are to run in the afternoon races.

Motivation   The sum of the energizing forces, both internal and external, to a person that account, in part, for certain behaviors.

Mouthpiece   A lawyer.

Move   To cheat using sleight of hand.

Muck   A cheating technique in which one or all of the cards the cheat has been dealt in a game are switched for previously palmed cards.

Mucker   (1) A cheater who uses palming and switching techniques. (2) In roulette, the second dealer who facilitates payoffs and cleans up checks.

Mug Punter   A gambler who does not have a rudimentary knowledge of the odds and probabilities in a game he is playing.

Multidimensional Scaling   A statistical technique that allows attitudinal data to be collected for several attributes in a manner that yields a single overall rating.

Multiple Action Blackjack   Version of blackjack that allows wagerers to play up to three hands at one time and to make three bets, all from the same deck.

Multiple Decks   A blackjack game played with two or more decks of cards.

Multiple Regression   A statistical technique that allows assessment of the relationship between an interval variable and two or more interval, ordinal, or nominal variables.

Multiple Slot Machines   Slot machines that accept one to eight coins and pay off winners in multiple fashions.

Multiplier   In regional economics, a term used to denote the change in an induced variable (gross national product, money supply, tourism spending) per unit change in an external variable (government spending, tax rates, building a casino).

Mystery Shopper   Hired or in-house person who poses as a guest, methodically samples the service and its delivery, observes the overall guest service operation, and then submits a report to management.

N

Nail   To catch someone cheating.

Nail Work   A cheating technique in which the cheat presses a thumb or fingernail into the edge of a card to leave a mark that can be seen across the table and felt when the cheat is dealing.

Name Credit System   Credit play system that allows the casino to issue markers in the pit, but does not allow redemptions in the pit.

National Gambling Impact and Policy Commission Act   Act that established a nine-member federal commission; impacts all types of gambling in the United States.

National Indian Gaming Association   Represents the Native American tribes in the United States that have gaming; located in Washington, DC.

National Restaurant Association (NRA)   The association representing restaurant owners and the restaurant industry.

Native American   A term referring to people who settled in the United States before Europeans arrived.

Natural   (1) In blackjack, a two-card count of twenty-one. (2) In craps, a seven or eleven on the come-out roll. (3) In baccarat, a two-card count of eight or nine.

NCRG   An abbreviation for the *National Center for Responsible Gaming*; a research and education foundation created by the gaming entertainment industry to fund gambling addiction research.

Necktying   A cheating technique in which the dealer tilts the front end of the deck upward to hide a second deal.

Needs   A person's physical and psychological desires.

NEVADA: PRISMS & PERSPECTIVES

Welcome to *Nevada: Prisms & Perspectives*, the latest version of the Nevada Historical Society's permanent exhibition in the Wilbur S. Shepperson Gallery. Design was by Howard Schureman of Riverside, California, and installation was by Gyford Productions of Reno. All of the interpretation and collections--artifacts, photographs and maps--come from the Nevada Historical Society.

Nevada: Prisms & Perspectives utilizes the Historical Society's collections to tell five crucial stories about life in the Silver State. Each story is complete in itself, but all five are intimately related to each other. Please join us in experiencing Nevada's fascinating heritage.

Living on the Land: Although the land of the eastern Sierra Nevada and Great Basin appears to be a hard place to survive in, people have been taking their living from the land here for over 10,000 years. Native Nevadans learned to live easily on the land, taking only what they needed and not hurting what they left. About 1,000 years ago in the southern part of the state, the Anazazi (the "Ancient Ones" in Hopi) built adobe towns and farmed the rich bottomlands of the Virgin and Muddy river valleys, until they moved on to the south and east. More recently, four major groups have occupied what is now Nevada. The Washoe are in the corner around Lake Tahoe, which is the center of their spiritual world. The Northern Paiute range stretches up into what is now Oregon and Idaho, and down to the southwest toward the Owens Valley. To the east the Western Shoshone fills the middle section, and the Southern Paiute range includes parts of both Nevada and Utah.

When Euroamericans began arriving in the Great Basin in the second quarter of the nineteenth century, they first sought wealth in the form of beaver pelts (to be used in making fashionable hats). As some came to stay, they turned to farming and ranching, both cattle and, later, sheep. By the last part of the century, traditional Native

American life was no longer possible in Nevada, and many of th
state's indigenous inhabitants turned to the new ranches and town
for jobs. Some women, in particular, adapted ancient arts to nev
markets. Most notable of these was the Washoe basketmaker, Dat
so-la-lee, who made her living in the first part of the twentiet
century selling her baskets as pieces of art. Today ranching an
farming continue to prosper in Nevada. In addition to cattle, shee
and dairy farming, favored products include alfalfa, garlic, potatoe
and onions.

Riches from the Earth: The Great Basin has been the source o
fabulous mineral wealth for hundreds of years. Native Nevadans fo
centuries mined salt and turquoise. More recently, prospector
heading back east from the first wave of the California Gold Rus
found traces of the yellow metal in streams on the eastern slope o
the Sierra. The real excitement began in 1859, however, with th
"Rush to Washoe," as thousands of former 49ers headed to th
booming Comstock Lode camps of Virginia City, Gold Hill an
Silver City.

Mining brought modern civilization and towns to Nevada. Nevad
silver and gold built the stock exchange in San Francisco, helped pa
for the Civil War and fostered statehood for Nevada in 1864. Camp
boomed and then went bust all over the state--from Treasure Hill t
Eureka to Austin to Belmont to Candelaria to Columbia to El Dorad
Canyon. Men and women from all the continents of the earth cam
to make their fortunes; the fortunate made a living. Then, for ove
twenty years, there was nothing, and the state almost blew away. I
1902 Tonopah in central Nevada suddenly boomed, followed in
few years by the even more fabulous Goldfield. About the sam
time, large-scale copper mining started in White Pine County.

Nevada has never really looked back. Industrial minerals of man
sorts, including uranium and oil, are found throughout the state
Gold mining has continued in many places for decades. Toda
Nevada is the largest producer of gold in the country, and mining i
still a major industry in the Silver State.

Passing Through: People have been getting across what is now Nevada, on their way to somewhere else, for decades. Interstate 80, in fact, just about a mile south of here, is the latest version of U.S. 40, which was the Victory Highway, which was built along the route of the Central Pacific end of the transcontinental railroad, which was along the path of the old wagon road the Donner Party took to get to California, which was also the route into the Sierra Nevada which took John C. Frémont and his party to Lake Tahoe, which was the path the Washoes used to move into the mountains from the north for the summer season. East of Reno and the Forty-Mile Desert, this modern superhighway follows the old Humboldt River route that brought so many pioneers to the Far West.

Further south, U.S. 50 follows the route explored by the Simpson expedition in 1859. Heading west, it generally follows the path of the Carson River, past Dayton and Genoa, the oldest Euroamerican settlements in Nevada, and then on to other passes across the Sierra-- Luther Pass, Big Trees Pass (Kingsbury Grade), and Carson Pass. In southern Nevada, Interstate 15 is the newest version of the old Arrowhead Highway, which first brought automobile tourists to Las Vegas. That highway paralleled the Union Pacific Railroad (originally the San Pedro, Los Angeles & Salt Lake), which carried freight for the mining camps of central Nevada and was responsible for creating Las Vegas, that singular oasis in the Mojave Desert. Even before the railroad, the route was the Old Spanish Trail.

Neon Nights: Everyone knows the truth about Nevada. It is a land of enchantment, offering fun, food, and instant wealth. The Corbett-Fitzsimmons fight in 1897 brought notoriety to the Silver State. Then speedy divorce--"Renovation"--as well as quickie marriages, kept the state's racy reputation alive. Gambling was made legal in Nevada in 1931 in order to support tourism and business in the face of the Great Depression.

The early casinos were rather dark and smoky. As soldiers and sailors came through Reno on the way to the coast during World

War II, a new prosperity hit the clubs and they began to expand and improve. With the growth of California after the war, the market took off and the clubs went right with it, creating the modern gambling meccas that beckon in the desert. Bright lights, architectural innovation, first-class entertainment, exciting games, great cuisine--all go into Neon Nights. They are here to enjoy.

The Federal Presence: Although Nevada is the seventh largest state in the Union, the federal government owns 87 percent of the land. That simple fact has made the federal presence central to the development of the Silver State in the twentieth century. The construction of Hoover Dam (1931-1935) brought abundant water and electrical power to Clark County in the south and sparked the transformation of Las Vegas from a division point on the railroad into a vast playground for adults and one of the fastest growing cities in the country. With World War II came thousands of men and women in the military services, passing through and staying to work in defense industries. Huge military bases sprouted up throughout the state. After the war, the testing of nuclear bombs spurred further growth. Even today, after the testing has ended, Nevada is facing federal pressure to become the storehouse for the nation's nuclear waste. Not only is the federal government the main landlord in Nevada, federal policies and actions have had a great impact on the state's growth and development.

The Nevada Historical Society is an agency of the Department of Cultural Affairs, Division of Museums and History. Please visit our sister museums:

Nevada State Museum, Carson City
Nevada State Railroad Museum, Carson City
East Ely Depot State Museum, Ely
Nevada State Museum and Historical Society, Las Vegas
Lost City Museum, Overton

Negative Swing   A period during which a loss is shown, even with a mathematical advantage.

Negotiation   The process in which two or more parties want to exchange goods or services and attempt to agree on a suitable exchange rate.

Neighbors   In roulette, numbers that are in proximity on the wheel.

Nepotism   The practice of hiring one's own relatives to work in the same organization.

Net Cash Receipts   The amount of cash and checks in the register drawer minus the amount of the initial cash bank.

Net Investment   The gross investment minus depreciation of capital goods.

Net Loss   The negative result of deducting gross expenses, including taxes, from gross revenues.

Net Profit   The gross profit minus operating expenses.

Networking   (1) Linking computers to communicate with each other. (2) People meeting others in their profession to help each other.

Net Worth   Total assets minus total liabilities.

New Product Development Process   Process used to evaluate, develop, and launch new products.

New York Craps   A form of bank craps played mostly in the eastern United States in which the player must pay a 5 percent commission for betting the box or off numbers.

Niche   A unique position that separates a product or organization from its competitors (e.g., adding an amusement park to a hotel, when no other competitors have one, creates a *niche* for the hotel).

Nickel   Five-dollar chips.

NIGA   An abbreviation for *National Indian Gaming Act*.

Night Audit   In accounting, the daily review of guest accounts against revenue center transaction information.

Night Auditor   In hotels, the employee who checks the accuracy of front office accounting records and compiles a daily summary of hotel financial data.

Night Shift   Work shift that generally takes place from eleven p.m. to seven a.m.

Ninety Days   In craps, the point nine.

No Brainer   A slang term for a decision that is so easy that a person could make it correctly without thinking.

No Dice   A craps term referring to a disallowed roll of the dice (usually because they failed to hit a wall or did not land straight).

Noir   A roulette term referring to a bet for the winning number to be black.

Noise   In the communication process, any disturbances that interfere with transmission of a message.

Nominal Scale   In creating a research design, the measurement instrument codes the responses as numbers solely for the purpose of identification (e.g., assigning "male" a "1" and "female" a "2" to distinguish the gender difference).

Nonaffiliate Reservation Network   Central reservation system that connects independent properties.

Nonautomated   A system of front office record keeping that exclusively uses handwritten forms.

Nonguaranteed Reservation   When the hotel agrees to hold a room until a stated time but no payment is received if the guest does not show up.

Nonguest Account   An account created to track the financial transactions of organizations that use the facilities of the hotel.

Nonguest Folio   A statement of transactions for a nonguest business or agency that has hotel charge purchase privileges.

Nonmonetary Compensation   Recompense other than money that includes items such as trips, awards, or recognition.

Nonprice Competition   A strategy in which price is fixed for everyone and therefore other factors must be used, such as advertising or product differentiation, as a basis for competition.

Nonverbal Communication   An aspect of communication that refers to meanings that are transmitted without words (e.g., when poker players watch their opponents' faces for positive or negative reactions to the cards).

No-Post Status   A guest who is not allowed to charge purchases to the room.

Normal Distribution   A statistical term that refers to the symmetrical, bell-shaped curve on which large numbers of data points form around the expected or average outcome. For example, if the odds are equal, a gambler would expect that half the time he would win and half the time he would lose. If these points were plotted on a graph, they would form a normal distribution around the midpoint.

Normative Influence   In organizational behavior, a natural process of groups of people is that they set and enforce their ideas of conduct (e.g., if a group of people go to the casino together, they will influence each other to stay longer and bet more).

Normative Social Influence   When a person allows behavior to be altered in order to meet the expectations of a person or group (e.g., Sam does not want to go to the casino but his wife does, so he goes to keep peace in the family).

Norms   Informal rules of conduct (e.g., in America, tips are expected, whereas in Japan, tipping is considered an insult).

Noser   Short for a drawer or bank that balanced at the end of the shift.

No-Show   A person who makes a reservation but does not cancel and does not show up.

NRA   An abbreviation for *National Restaurant Association*.

Number Two Man   A cheating move in which the dealer deals the second card from the top.

Nut   (1) Overhead expenses. (2) The amount a casino must make to break even.

O

Objective   A strategic planning term that refers to the measurable goal that an organization plans to reach in a specific time frame (e.g., a company plans a 5 percent growth rate by next January).

Observational Learning   When people learn by watching others (e.g., people watch the table play in order to learn the game before sitting down to play).

Occupancy Data   In casinos, the actual count of individual machine usage.

Occupancy Percentage   A statistical term that shows the ratio of the number of rooms sold to rooms available for sale during a specific period of time, expressed as a percentage.

Occupancy Report   Front-office statement that shows which rooms were sold and inhabited.

Occupied   The front-office term for a room in which a guest is currently registered.

Octant   In roulette, a term referring to a group of any five numbers that are physically adjacent around the wheel.

Odds   Ratio or probability that one event will happen over another.

Odd Splitters   Dice that are misspotted to make it impossible for the shooter to roll either of the odd point numbers, five or nine.

Off   In craps, a term that a bet is off or not in action for a specific roll of the dice.

Office   Any kind of secret sign given between cheats.

Off-Number Bet   In craps, a bet that the shooter will, or will not, throw a specified number other than her point before throwing a seven.

Off Numbers   In craps, the box numbers including four, five, six, eight, nine, and ten.

Off the Board   An event that is declared ineligible for wagering that may result from uncertainty caused by injury to a key player.

Off the Rail   Observing a gambling game from behind the players but not playing.

Off the Square   Honest.

Off the Street   Getting a job without knowing anyone at the casino, as in "Joe came in *off the street.*"

Off the Top   In card games, the beginning of the deck or shoe immediately after the shuffle.

Off-Track Betting   Betting that takes place somewhere other than at the actual racetrack.

Oligopoly   In economics, a term referring to the competitive environment in which a few large corporations control the market.

On-Change   A front-office term signifying that a guest has departed but the room needs to be cleaned and prepared for the new guest.

One-Armed Bandit   Slot machine.

One Big One   One thousand dollars.

One-Down   In craps, announcement by the stickperson that one die has fallen off the table.

One-Eyed Jack   In poker, a term referring to when the jack of hearts and spades are used as wild cards.

One-Number Bet   In craps, a bet that a specific number will or will not be thrown before another number.

One-Roll Bet   In craps, a term referring to a wager that will be decided on the next roll of the dice.

Online   A computer term referring to hardware that is capable of interacting directly with the central processing unit.

On the Rail   A person who watches, but does not play, a game.

On the Square   Fair, honest.

On the Stick   In craps, a dealers' term referring to the rotation of deal-ers after a work break when the new stickman begins the game or is *on the stick.*

On the Up-and-Up   Straight, honest game.

On the Wall   A criminal's term for the person who is assigned to be the lookout for approaching police.

OOO   An abbreviation for *out of order.*

Open   (1) In hotels, a term referring to the fact that rooms are still available. (2) In poker, the beginning bet of the game.

Open Craps   When side bets among the players are permitted.

Open-Door Policy   Employee problem resolution process in which the workers can go directly to higher level managers.

Open-Ended Questions   In research, a term referring to the type of questions in which respondents are free to reply in their own words.

Open-End Straight   In poker, when the first four cards dealt are in numerical sequence and a fifth card is needed for the bottom or top to make a straight.

Opener   (1) In poker, when the minimum hand needed to begin a poker pot is usually a pair of jacks or better. (2) A casino term that refers to the slip of paper in the chip tray or check bank showing the amount of chip value for opening the game.

Open Up   (1) A casino term to start a game. (2) Usually in a criminal context, a person who gives information or *opens up* with some pressure.

Operant Conditioning   A learning theory that views behavior as a re-action to a stimulus because of expected reinforcement; for example, Sally sees a slot machine at the end of the aisle, pulls the lever, and receives ten dollars. The next time this situation occurs, Sally will be likely to try again because she was rewarded with ten dollars the last time.

Operating Costs   In management, money needed to pay the day-to-day expenses of a corporation.

Opinion Leaders   People who are looked to for advice by others; for example, Sam always wins at poker so people ask him for sugges-tions on improving their game.

Optimization Models   In economics, a statistical method for analyz-ing data by maximizing some criteria.

Option   Choice of actions.

Order for Credit A two-part document used by a pit floor supervisor to send a credit of chips, tokens, coin, and/or markers from a specific gaming table to the casino cage.

Order for Fill A two-part document used by a pit floor supervisor to inform the casino cage that a specific table is in need of a table fill of specific chip denominations.

Ordinal Scale In research, a term referring to the measurement of responses in which numbers are assigned on the basis of some order (one to five, best to worst).

Organizational Culture The pattern of beliefs and expectations shared by organizational members (e.g., in the 1800s, the organizational culture in casinos was to obey the owner without question).

Organizational Structure In management, the formally designed framework of authority and task relationships in an organization.

Organization Chart In management, a term referring to the diagram of relationships between positions within an organization.

Orientation Process of introducing a new employee to the job and organization.

OTB An abbreviation for *off-track betting*.

Our Money A term used to describe the situation in which a winning player is believed by casino personnel to be placing her wagers with money that has been won from the casino.

Out in Front When a player wins more than she loses.

Outlier In research, a term referring to a response or data point that is radically different from the rest of the responses.

Out of Order (OOO) A guestroom that cannot be used.

Outside In roulette, the bets placed outside the table layout of the boxes for the thirty-seven or thirty-eight numbers.

Outside Man (1) A casino employee who observes from outside the pit. (2) Someone who is part of a cheating team.

Outside Ticket A keno ticket, normally computer-generated, that is presented to the player after the inside ticket and wager are received; indicates the numbers selected, the amount of the wager, and the game number.

Outside Work A cheating term that refers to anything done to the surface of the dice.

Overage When the total of cash and checks in a register is greater than the initial bank plus net cash receipts.

Overboard   To be unable to pay off on gambling debts.

Overbooking   When a service organization accepts reservations that outnumber available units.

Overhead   Expenses that are needed to maintain the day-to-day functions of the firm.

Overlay   (1) In betting, a development when the odds are greater than they should be. (2) A player who bets more than his bankroll.

P

Pack   An unopened deck of fifty-two cards plus two jokers.

Package   (1) A cheating term referring to a prestacked deck that is swapped for the actual playing cards. (2) In tourism, a prepaid tour that includes transportation, lodging, and usually meals, transfers, sightseeing, or car rentals.

Package Plan Rate   A special room rate that includes other meals, activities, or events.

Pack Up   To stop playing and leave the game.

Pad   (1) Payroll. (2) The colored compartments of a roulette wheel.

Paddle   The plastic slat that dealers use to push paper money into the drop box.

Pad Roll   A cheating technique of throwing the dice so that they roll without spinning.

Paid Out   In lodging, an accounting term referring to the cash disbursed by the hotel on behalf of a guest and charged to the guest's account.

Pai-Gow   An oriental table game using thirty-two domino-type playing pieces and dice; there are seven players and a banker who each get a stack of four dominoes and the object of the game is to split the dominoes into two sets, which have the highest possible ranking.

Pai-Gow Poker   A version of poker that uses seven cards to make a five-card high hand and a two-card, second best hand. These hands are played against the house's hand. A player must win both hands to win or lose both hands to lose. Otherwise, it is a tie, or a push. Because this is an even game, a vigorish is charged on all winning hands.

Paint   A jack, queen, or king (sometimes a ten).

Painter   A card cheat who specializes in daubing the cards during play.

Pair   (1) In European roulette, a bet on even. (2) In poker, a hand containing two cards of the same value.

Pair Splitting   In blackjack, a hand that contains two cards of the same value that can be split or separated and bet as two new separate hands.

Palette   A wooden palette with a long, thin handle used by baccarat and chemin de fer dealers to move the cash and chips around.

Palm   A cheating technique that uses sleight of hand by picking up the cards from the table on a new deal and slipping the unwanted cards into the hollow of the palm of one's hand.

Pan   Card game grouped under the generic name of "rummy."

Panhandler   A person who asks for money from players.

Paper   (1) A cheating term referring to cards that are marked on the back prior to play. (2) Money.

Par   In slot machines, it refers to the expected hold of the machine.

Pari-mutuel   Races in which all bets are pooled and the winner is paid off according to the number of winners, minus a standard track deduction.

Parity   In management, compensation term referring to the idea that each person who has responsibility to perform a task should have equivalent authority and/or pay to the others in similar jobs.

Parlay   (1) A cumulative bet in which all monies won from one wager are automatically bet again. (2) To enlarge an original bankroll, as in "he *parlayed* one hundred dollars into one thousand dollars."

Partage (le Partage)   In European roulette, there are two options for play when the ball lands on 0 or 00; the partage option means that the player simply divides the chips and keeps half.

Partnership   A legal term referring to an unincorporated firm owned by two or more persons.

Party   A term used by cheats to signify opportunities for a scam.

Pass   (1) In craps, a bet that a shooter will throw a seven on the come out roll. (2) In craps, when a shooter wins a seven or eleven on the initial throw of the dice or makes her point on a subsequent roll.

Passe   In European roulette, a bet on the high numbers, nineteen to thirty-six.

Passers   A cheating term referring to the crooked dice that tend to make more passes than fair dice.

Pass-Line (1) In craps, the area of table layout on which the pass bets are made. (2) In craps, a basic wager in which the player is betting with the shooter.

Past-Posting An illegal practice of attempting to place a bet after the results are known.

Pat A poker term referring to a hand that is good enough as it stands or the fact that no additional cards are needed for the hand.

Pathological Gambling According to the American Psychiatric Association, it is an official mental disease or disorder, characterized by the inability to stop wagering.

Pay The compensation that employees receive.

Payline The centerline in the window of a slot machine on which the payoff symbols appear.

Payoff (1) The collection of a bet. (2) Any final event.

Payoff Odds Ratio at which any bet is paid; for example, if one beats the dealer in blackjack, the payoff odds are one to one, which means that for every dollar bet, the player will receive a dollar return.

Payout In casinos, customer's winnings.

Payout Interval How fast the player is paid; in casinos, payouts are immediate; in other forms of gambling, intervals vary (e.g., a forty-million-dollar lottery can be paid over 20 years).

Payout Schedule A schedule that is posted or distributed by the casino to indicate to players the amount to be paid out for certain winning wagers; common to slot machines as well as games like keno and bingo.

Pay the Board When the house elects to pay every player at the table, regardless of count total.

PBX Part of the communication's equipment; the hotel's telephone switchboard equipment.

PC (1) A casino management term referring to the percentage of money put down the drop box and money given out of the rack to determine winnings and losses. (2) A casino term that relates to the percentage the house has as an advantage over the player.

PC Dice In cheating equipment, crooked dice that give a cheat an advantage but do not win every time.

Peek Freak Disparaging term that describes a hole card player.

Peeking A cheating technique in which the thumb presses down and to the left of the top card, pushing it against the fingers on the opposite corner of the deck so that the top card buckles just enough for the dealer to get a glimpse of the inner corner of the card.

Peek the Poke   A cheater's term to describe the effort she must expend to determine how much cash is in a mark's wallet.

Peg   (1) In craps, indicates a point with a puck or marker on the number. (2) To typecast a person.

Pegging   Using a small thumbtack, the cheater pricks certain cards in a spot with the idea to "peg" the card without penetrating all the way through so that when dealing, the cheater can feel the cards.

Pencil   A person having the juice (power) to write comps.

Penny Ante   Wagers made for extremely small stakes.

Pepper   An extremely green or naive victim of gambling cheats.

Perceived Risk   How a person views the potential negative consequences of an action; for example, a habitual gambler will always acknowledge the money won and ignore the money lost, which allows him to continue hoping for the big jackpot. Therefore, he diminishes the perceived risk of losing so that he can rationalize gambling.

Percentage   (1) House advantage expressed as a percentage. (2) In cheating, dice that alter the advantage.

Percentage Dice   Gaffed dice that tilt the odds in the cheat's favor but do not guarantee a win.

Percentage Game   A banking game in which an advantage is obtained through relatively disproportionate odds.

Percentage Tops and Bottoms   In cheating, a pair of altered, misspotted dice that usually have a 2 or a 5 twice on the die.

Perception   A psychological term referring to the process by which stimuli are selected, organized, and interpreted; for example, gamblers who see themselves as lucky may only perceive the wins and not the losses. This is a perceptual distortion.

Perfects   Casino quality dice that are perfect cubes to a tolerance of 1/5,000 of an inch.

Performance   A management term referring to the process of expending effort to reach individual or organizational goals.

Performance Appraisal   A management term referring to the review of employee job performance in relation to job standards and expectations.

Performance Feedback   A management communication tool that gives evaluative information about an employee's progress toward a specific goal.

Personality A person's psychological makeup, which influences her reactions to the environment (e.g., security people who sit in a room alone and watch the monitors for eight hours should not be people who are "social animals"—therefore, the personality traits for a security monitor person would be a solitary person who pays a great deal of attention to details).

Personal Selling A marketing tool used in person-to-person communication.

Persuasion A psychological tool that is an active attempt to change a person's attitude.

Philadelphia Layout The first bank craps layout to give the players an opportunity to bet the dice to win and lose.

Philistines Loan sharks.

Phoebe In craps, the point five.

Phony (1) In cheating, crooked dice. (2) A person who is a fake.

Physical Distribution A marketing term referring to the process of physically moving goods from source of supply to point of consumption.

PIA (1) An acronym for *paid in advance*. (2) A hotelier's term for a guest who pays in cash during registration.

Picasso A card cheater who specializes in daubing the cards during play.

Pick-and-Pay A dealer's method of turning over a player's cards, paying, or taking the bets, and picking up that hand before proceeding to the next player's hand.

Pickup Stack The technique of stacking certain cards in the process of picking up the cards lying face up from the previous round of play.

Picture Cards In a deck of cards, the face cards (jack, queen, king).

Piece A slang term for a share of the profits.

Piece of Cake An expression referring to a simple, easy, or pleasant job.

Pigeon A cheater's jargon for a victim in a gambling scam.

Piker A gambler who makes small bets opposite big bettors because the bank will beat the big player.

PIMS An abbreviation for *profit impact on market share*.

Pinch A casino term referring to the instance when a person tries to illegally remove part, or all, of a wager.

Pinch and Press A cheating technique in which a player adds or subtracts from her bet after seeing her cards.

Pinching   Increasing or decreasing a bet after completion of play.

Pips   A cheating scam in which the design on the cards indicates its denomination.

Pit   In the casino layout, a single grouping of adjacent table games.

Pit Boss   In the casino management hierarchy, the most senior gaming supervisor in the pit who supervises play and the activities of several floorpersons.

Pitch Game   Single- or double-deck blackjack in which the dealer deals the cards from his hand.

Pit Clerk   An employee who is dedicated to a particular pit, but generally reports to the casino cage and is independent of casino supervisory personnel; responsibilities include input of information resulting in the generation of fill, credit, and marker transactions corresponding to the tables within the pit.

Pit Stand   The desk stand for floorpersons' use in writing or phoning while they are in the pit.

Pizza   In baccarat, a random method of mixing cards prior to shuffling.

Place Bet   In craps, a bet on the result of a throw when the shooter is trying for a point.

Plaques   Used primarily in casinos outside the United States; rectangular in shape and used in the same way as cheques.

Play   A casino term referring to the betting or action.

Play Best Hand   Two or more poker players acting in collusion, signaling each other's hands, and having the strongest player stay in the pot while the others drop out.

Player   A casino term referring to the gambler, bettor, or patron.

Player Hand   In baccarat, one of the two betting propositions.

Player's Advantage   A gambling term referring to the percent of money bet that a player can expect to win in the long run.

Player's Bias   A casino term referring to the bias in the ordering of a deck or shoe of cards when it favors the player.

Player Tracking System   (1) In slots, a computer software program that tracks all the coins put into the machines and the betting patterns they use. (2) A system in which the supervisors rate the player according to his action on the table games.

Pleasure Principle   A psychological theory that says a person's behavior is motivated by the desire to maximize pleasure and avoid pain.

Plug   (1) The same as slug. (2) A prearranged group of cards or a group of cards rich in low or high cards.

Plus Count   In card counting for blackjack, when the counter believes that there is an excess of ten value cards in proportion to low value cards.

PMS   An abbreviation for *property management systems*; a system of storing and retrieving information on reservations, room availability, and room rates; may also interface with outlets (bars, restaurants, etc.) for recording guest charges.

Pocket   In roulette, a part of the equipment that refers to the compartments on the roulette wheel in which the ball falls.

Point   In craps play, when a shooter tries to throw the dice so that a four, five, six, eight, nine, or ten on the come-out roll and then tries to roll the same number before throwing a seven.

Point Bet   In craps, a bet whether or not the point will be made.

Point Count   In blackjack, a card counter's term for the player's evaluation of the odds via a tally of assigned points of each card.

Point Numbers   In craps, a four, five, six, eight, nine, or ten.

Point of Sale (POS)   (1) Computerized system that allows bars to set drink prices according to the specific ingredients served. (2) Computerized cash register.

Point Spread   A handicap in the form of points added by oddsmakers to the scores of teams in games of predictable outcomes that are the object of betting.

Poke   Wallet.

Poker   A card game in which the objective is to win the pot by either exposing the best hand at the final showdown, or by being the last player left in the hand after forcing the other players out by making a final bet that no other player calls.

Policy   In management, a statement used as a decision-making guide to implement a strategic plan.

Polly   Politician.

Pontoon   Another name for blackjack, twenty-one, or the French vingt-et-un.

Population   A research term referring to all of the possibilities in a selected group.

Portfolio Analysis   A marketing process regarding which markets or products should be maintained, expanded, or phased out.

POS An abbreviation for *point of sale*.

Positioning A marketing term referring to the fit of a product to a segment of the market so that it is perceived as different from the competition.

Positive Deck A card counter's term referring to when the remaining cards in the deck have a favorable plus count.

Positive Reinforcement A psychological learning term referring to the fact that rewards provided by the environment strengthen responses to the stimuli; for example, slot machines provide intermittent positive reinforcements in the form of payouts so that people will bet more.

Posting A hotel term referring to the process of recording transactions on a guest folio.

Pot Total money or chips in a pool to be taken by the winning player(s).

Pound Five dollars.

Power Potential to influence the behavior of others.

Preferential A casino move to break up a positive count for a card counter in which the dealer shuffles the deck.

Premium A pricing term that is an offer of an item or service either for free or at a low price, as an extra incentive for purchasers.

Premium House A casino that caters to "high rollers" or people who habitually bet a lot of money.

Premium Player A casino term referring to a person who consistently bets high stakes; commonly called a "high roller."

Pre-Registration In lodging, a process in which parts of the registration are completed before the guest arrives.

Present Value A financial term referring to today's value for assets that yield a stream of income over time.

Press A gambling term referring to doubling a bet.

Press-a-Bet A gambling term referring to increasing a bet after a win.

Press Release A marketing term referring to the factual information released to the press.

Prestige Pricing A marketing term referring to the practice of pricing a product high so that a consumer will perceive quality and status.

Preventive Maintenance In the engineering department, maintenance should be performed at regularly scheduled intervals to minimize equipment failure and prolong the operating life of equipment.

Price (1) In casino marketing, a term denoted by the percentage of the gross amount wagered (handle) retained by the operators and is equivalent to the losses incurred by all gamblers over a period of time. (2) The value a willing buyer will exchange for goods or services.

Price Elasticity An economic term quantifying the degree to which quantity demanded by buyers responds to a price change.

Price Flexibility An economic term describing the market condition when the immediate price change depends on changes in supply or demand (e.g., auctions).

Price Index An economic term used by the government or industry to evaluate the average price of a bundle of goods so that prices can be compared over time.

Primary Data A research term describing the information collected for the express purpose of answering the question at hand.

Private Game Any game that has no houseman or banker, and in which no charge is extracted for the privilege of playing.

Probability A statistical term describing the likelihood that one among a number of possible outcomes of an event will occur.

Probability Sample A research term describing the idea that each subject in the population has an equal chance of being selected.

Procedure Casino management policies or guides for performing planned activities that occur regularly.

Product Differentiation A marketing term evaluating the characteristics that make a product different from its competitors.

Production Function An economic term specifying the amount of output that can be achieved with given inputs.

Productivity A management term referring to the ratio of output to inputs.

Product Life Cycle A theory that suggests products and services pass through four developmental stages: introduction, growth, maturity, and decline.

Product Positioning A marketing term describing the traits that allow the product to meet a customer's perceived needs while separating it from competitors.

Profit An accounting term quantified as sales revenue minus costs, properly chargeable against the goods sold.

Profit Center   A strategic management term for a highly autonomous unit given broad decision-making authority for its own operations.

Profit Impact on Market Share   A strategic marketing process that gathers data from a number of corporations to establish a relationship between a variety of business factors and measure organizational performance.

Profit Sharing   A compensation program in which certain employees can receive a portion of organizational profits.

Progression   A betting sequence in which the player gambles an incremental increase in the wager after decisions.

Progressive Slot Machine   An individual slot machine, or one linked to a group of machines, in which the jackpot amount increases with each coin wagered by the player(s).

Promotion   A strategic marketing process to coordinate seller-initiated efforts to set up channels of information and persuasion to sell services or to promote an idea.

Prop   (1) Any unusual type of wager that appears to favor both players equally. (2) In craps, short for proposition bets.

Prop Bets   Proposition bets.

Property Management System   A hotel term for the computer software that supports front-office and back-office activities.

Prop Hustler   A grafter who specializes in luring victims into bets in which they have little or no chance of winning.

Proposition Bets   In craps, a bet on long shots; bets handled by the stickman on a craps game, like the hardway bets, a one roll, or craps.

Prospect   Potential buyer.

Prove   To cut checks in a certain manner to verify accuracy.

Prove a Hand   To reconstruct the hands just previously picked up in order to verify a decision.

Psychographics   A strategic marketing term referring to the use of psychological and sociological factors to develop groups of people with common interests (e.g., the MGM Grand in Las Vegas used *psychographic* information about families to develop a themed amusement park).

Publicity   A marketing communications term that refers to the press coverage or other disseminated information that is not paid directly to the media and is not controlled by the corporation.

Puck   Part of the craps table equipment that is a marker used to indicate the point number and whether odds are on or off on the come-out roll.

Pull Down   In craps, when a player takes back all or part of a wager just won rather than let it continue for the next roll.

Pull Through   A sleight of hand move that appears to be a cut made just after a shuffle; it separates the two halves of the deck and replaces them as they were before the shuffle.

Pull Up   A scam artist's term for a possible mark who loses interest.

Pull Up a Play   A cheating signal between partners calling a play in counting or hole-card action.

Punchy   Mentally slow.

Punk   (1) Slang term referring to a novice. (2) Slang term referring to a small-time gambler or crook.

Punter   In baccarat or chemin de fer, the player or shooter.

Punto Banco   A table game; also known as *baccarat, chemin de fer, American baccarat, Nevada baccarat.*

Purse Drawer   The bottom part of the casino table where a drawer is located that holds the table accessories and dealer's purse.

Push   A standoff or tie between the player and the dealer in which neither wins nor loses.

Put Bet   In craps, a wager that may be made at any time on any of the numbers, 4, 5, 6, 8, 9, 10 that wins if the number on which the wager was placed is thrown before a 7 appears and loses if a 7 is thrown before that number; it may not be taken down after the next roll of the dice.

Put On the Send   A scam artist's term referring to sending a mark home to get more money.

Put Up   A gambling term referring to the situation in which a player makes a bet on behalf of the dealer.

Put the Bite On   Slang term referring to someone who wants to borrow money.

Put the Finger On   Slang term referring to secretly identifying criminals to the police.

Put the Horns On   Slang for a bad luck omen to a player.

Put the Lid On   (1) When a casino closes a table by covering the rack with a locked lid. (2) Person stops talking and becomes quiet.

Put the Pressure On   Coercion.

Q

Qualified Player   A rated player; less than a premium player who is eligible for comps.

Quality Circles   A management practice in which work groups meet regularly to discuss, investigate, and correct quality problems.

Quality of Life   A sociological term referring to an emphasis on the relationships and concern for others that indicate how happy people are with their lives.

Quarters   Twenty-five dollar table checks.

Queer   (1) Slang for counterfeit money. (2) A slang term for upsetting someone's plans. (3) Strange. (4) Slang term for someone who is gay or lesbian.

Queuing Models   A mathematical analysis of the costs of waiting lines.

Quinella   Used in racing, when the bettor must pick the first two horses, or dogs, that cross the finish line.

R

Rabbit   (1) A person who scares easily. (2) A sucker.

Rabbit Ears   A term used to describe the two tubes into which the winning balls are blown on a keno game; the tubes allow the numbers on the balls to be displayed to players as well as employees.

Race Book   A business that accepts wagers on horse, or other, races.

Rack   A piece of equipment for the tables that is a rectangular metal tray containing the table checks and silver, and lies flat in the middle of the table next to the dealer.

Rack Rate   A hotel term that refers to the standard or full-price rates established by the property.

Raffle   A lottery.

Rail   (1) A casino term referring to the carpeted area bordering the gaming tables. (2) In roulette, the wheel groove on which the ball spins.

Railbird   A thief who steals unaware players' gaming chips from the edge, or "rail," of the table.

Raise   In poker, when a player bets more than the previous player and forces all opponents to match the higher stakes or drop out of the game.

Rake   Croupier's stick.

Rake-Off   A percentage taken by the casino as a commission from customers playing poker.

Random Distribution   A mathematical probability in which everything has an equal opportunity to be selected.

Random Number Generator   A statistical process in which each number has an equal probability of being selected by a computer; often used in slot machines.

Rank   The face value of a card.

Rat Hole   A cheater's place to hide illegally obtained chips or money.

Rating   A casino term referring to the measure of a player's potential value as a casino customer for the purpose of allocating complimentaries.

Rating Slip   (1) A sheet that indicates a player's activity for comps. (2) A record of a dealer's performance.

Ratio Analysis   Financial data expressed in the form of a comparison in order to evaluate organizational performance.

Rats   Dice.

Readable Dealer   A casino term for a dealer whose hole card can be spotted by a person in a casino.

Readers   A cheater's glasses or lenses used to read marked cards.

Ready a Tray   A casino term referring to the way dealers organize the tray so that a supervisor can count the content of the chip tray from a distance.

Ready Up   Prepare.

Real Dough   Large quantity of money.

Real Estate Investment Trust (REIT)   A method that allows small investors to combine their funds and protects them from double taxation that is levied against an ordinary corporation or trust; designed to facilitate investment in real estate as a mutual fund facilitates investment in securities.

Real Income   In economics, income that is adjusted for inflation.

Real Work   A cheater's slang for genuine inside information of the correct way to perform a cheating move or scam.

Recruitment   An organization's efforts to generate a list of job applicants.

Red   In roulette, a bet paying one to one.

Red-Dog   A casino table game in which players bet that the third card drawn falls between the values of two previously drawn cards.

Reds   Five-dollar table cheques or chips.

Reel Strip Listing   Arrangement of the symbols and spaces on the slot machine reel strips.

Reel Strip Settings   In casinos, the payout percentages that are preset in the slot machines.

Reel Timing   In slots, a player's attempt to time the spin of the reels and set them in motion so that they come to rest in desired positions.

Reference Groups   In consumer behavior, groups that set behavior standards to which other individuals adhere.

Registration   The procedure when an incoming guest signs the forms to contract for their stay.

Reg 6-A   The Federal Banking Secrecy Act of 1985, which requires casinos to record and get positive identification from all players buying in more than $10,000 in a twenty-four-hour period.

Regulation   The government laws or rules designed to change the behavior of firms or organizations.

REIT   An abbreviation for *real estate investment trust.*

Relationship Marketing   Emphasizes the importance of building long-term relationships with individual customers and with other organizations in the distribution chain.

Relay   A person who transmits signals from one person to another in a casino.

Reliability   (1) A research design question referring to the likelihood that the results can be duplicated again, with similar results. (2) The way a product or service fulfills its intended function.

Relief Dealer   A casino term referring to the new dealer who takes the place of the table dealer so she can take a break.

Rembrandt   A card cheater who specializes in daubing the cards during play.

Renege   Refuse to pay a wager or debt.

Reorder Point   Point at which an item needs to be reordered so as not to run out of it before the next delivery is received.

Repositioning   Using various promotional programs and physical changes in the product/service mix to change the image of an organization or product in customers' minds.

Research Design   Plan for a study that guides the collection and analysis of the data.

Research Process   A sequence of steps in the design and implementation of an experiment.

Reservation   An agreement between a guest and a business to hold a specific type of room or table for a specified date and length of time.

Resources   A strategic management term referring to the organization's people, capital, technology, clients, and time.

Respin   (1) In roulette, where the ball rolls on the wheel. (2) On a big six wheel, when the clapper stops on top of a peg, requiring a second spin.

Responsible Gaming   Strategies employed by the gaming entertainment industry to mitigate pathological and underage gambling, including prevention, education, and awareness programs for employees, customers, and local communities.

Responsibilities   An employee's assigned tasks, duties, and obligations to achieve expected performance results.

Restructuring   A strategic management term referring to alterations in the organizational chart for more efficient distribution of resources.

Result Player   A gambler who tells you how you should have made your bet or play after the decision has been made.

Retail   A type of business that involves the majority of the sale of goods and services directly to consumers for their personal, family, or household use.

Return   In gambling, the percentage of total money that is paid out to the customers.

Return on Assets (ROA)   A financial performance ratio based on net sales, net profits, and total assets.

Return on Investment (ROI)   A financial ratio that compares net income to stockholders' equity.

Revenue   (1) A financial term referring to the money earned by a business operation or income. (2) From the casino point of view, collective losses of gamblers.

Revolutions   A casino term referring to each time a wheel or reel spins one complete circle.

Rev Par   Revenue per available room.

Reward Power   A management term referring to the ability of a manager to distribute bonuses.

RFB   A casino term for the ultimate comp: free room, meals, and drinks.

Rhythm Play   The method used by players to attempt to control the slot machine combinations by carefully timing the pull of the handle.

Rich   A card counter's term referring to a shoe with a larger than normal percentage of a certain value of cards present.

Rich Environment   A service setting, environment, or servicescape in which more information is available for processing by guests.

Ride (the Action)   A victim tolerates a hustler's cheating actions without complaining because he is unaware that anything dishonest is happening.

Rien Ne Va Plus   In roulette, the croupier's call that ends betting on one spin of the wheel.

Riffle   A dealer's term referring to a method of shuffling cards by dividing the deck in two and intermingling the two sections.

Rig   A cheating maneuver to fix or prearrange a game's outcome.

Right Bettor   In craps, when a player bets the shooter will make his point.

Ring In   To introduce crooked gaming equipment into a game.

Ring in One's Nose   To be losing heavily and betting high, hoping to get even.

Rip   A cheating maneuver to switch dice.

Rip and Tear   To cheat without fear of the consequences.

Ripe   (1) Ready to make a loan. (2) Novice primed to be taken.

Rip In   In craps, to switch dice into a game.

Risk   Conditions in which the decision maker has to estimate the likelihood of certain outcomes.

Risk of Ruin   The probability that the gambler will tap out or lose his entire bankroll within a defined period or before achieving a specified goal.

Riverboat   A type of casino that floats on water.

ROA   An abbreviation for *return on assets*.

Road Hustler   A cheat who travels around looking for a game.

Road Mob   A team of card or dice cheats who travel around the country looking for games to cheat in.

Rob   To cheat the players in a game of chance.

Rock   A player who refuses to lend money.

Rod   Handgun.

ROI   An abbreviation for *return on investments*.

Role   A sociological term referring to a set of behavior patterns expected of someone occupying a given position in a social unit (e.g., the *role* of the breadwinner of a family is to bring home the money).

Roll   (1) A criminal move to steal from a person while they are asleep or intoxicated. (2) In craps, the throwing of the dice.

Roller   (1) In cards, the weight that holds the cards against the shoe. (2) Player or gambler.

Rolling Full Bloom   Fast paced, high stakes game.

Rolling the Bones   A player's term for shooting craps.

Rolling the Deck   A method of cheating at blackjack whereby the dealer secretly turns the deck over so the used face-up cards on the bottom are redealt.

Roll Over   (1) Slang for a criminal partner who tells the police what she knows. (2) In accounting, when an investment such as a certificate of deposit comes due and is automatically reinvested. (3) In casino accounting, paying off old markers with newly issued credit instruments.

Room Occupancy Percentage   A key operating ratio for hotels that is calculated by finding the number of rooms occupied and dividing by rooms available.

Rooms Division   A hotel department that includes the front office, reservations, telephone switchboard, housekeeping, uniformed service departments and functions.

Rope   Cheat.

Rope In   A scam artist's term for luring a mark into a swindle.

Roper   A hustler who recruits victims for gambling scams.

Roscoe   Handgun.

Rotation   The direction a wheel is spun.

Rouge   In roulette, a bet on red.

Rouge et Noir   French casino game; also called *Trente et Quarante* or *Thirty and Forty*.

Rough It Up   A gambling term meaning to bet heavily.

Roulette   A casino table game in which players bet on one or a combination of thirty-eight numbers, in which a small white ball is spun against a horizontal rotating wheel and it lands on the winning number.

Round   To cause someone to turn around to keep him from seeing a cheating move performed by one's partner.

Royal Flush   In poker, the highest possible hand that includes a ten, jack, queen, king, and ace, all in the same suit.

Rubber Band   A management system of assigning dealers to table games after the break when the dealers are not assigned a specific table.

Rug Joint   A plush gambling house.

Rule   An explicit statement that dictates what is acceptable.

Rumble   To discover crooked dealings.

Run   Length of time.

Run Down   Small, regulation-sized stacks of cheques; easily counted from a distance.

Runners   In keno, the casino personnel who pick up a customer's ticket and wager from anywhere in the casino hotel and take it to the keno booth.

Running Count   A card counter's cumulative value of all cards played at any given time; based on a preassigned value for each card.

Running Flat   For any gambling establishment, to be operating crookedly.

Run of the House   A hotel term to guarantee a firm price that applies to any room in the house.

Runt   In poker, a hand of less than one pair.

Run Up   To rearrange the cards while shuffling them so that a favorable hand will fall to one of the players.

Russian Service   Restaurant service in which the entrée, vegetables, and starches are served from a platter onto the diner's plate by a waiter.

S

Sabot   A piece of equipment on table games called a *dealing shoe*.

Sabre   Name of a commonly used airline reservation system.

Salary   An accounting term referring to a consistent payment for work rendered.

Sales Promotion   A paid marketing communication that stimulates short-term consumer purchases.

Salle Privée   In Europe, a private salon in the casino reserved for high-stakes games.

Sandbag Poker   A betting technique in which two players have a third in between them and keep raising without any consideration for the middle player.

Sand Work   A cheater's method of marking the backs of cards with very fine sandpaper.

Satisficing   A type of management decision process in which the adopted decision meets previously established minimum criteria, even when further research might reveal a better alternative.

Sawbuck   Ten dollars.

Sawdust Joint   Low budget or low roller casino.

Saw Tooth Edge Work   Dice that have been gaffed by placing small cuts on certain edges to retard the roll of the dice when they roll over these edges and thereby affect the odds.

SBU   An abbreviation for *strategic business unit*.

Scalar Principle   Concept that organizations should have a chain of authority and communication that runs from top to bottom and should be followed by managers and subordinates.

Scam   A method for cheating a gambling opponent.

Score   (1) A dealer's term for a bigger than normal tip night. (2) In general, a gambler's term for winning big. (3) In craps, to win. (4) Slang term for buying illegal drugs. (5) A cheater's term for the proceeds of a con game.

Score a Big Touch   To cheat a player out of a large amount of money.

Scratch   (1) Money. (2) In blackjack, the scraping motion of the cards a player uses to request a hit or take another card.

Screen Out   To cover up or misdirect attention away from a crooked gambling move.

SDS System   A computerized slot tracking system in which the player inserts a plastic card into a "reader" to record how long he plays and how much money he deposits into the machine to get credit for his playing time.

Seat of the Pants   Slang for making decisions based on intuition.

Seasonal Variations   A management term referring to the fluctuations of a variable that occur regularly during a yearly cycle.

Secondary Data   A statistical term referring to information that is not gathered for the immediate study at hand but for some other purpose.

Second Base   In a table game, the name of the position of the player sitting near the center of the table.

91

Second Dealer   A dealer who deals the second card from the deck when she appears to be dealing the top card.

Seconds   A cheating move when a dealer does not deal the top cards from the deck.

Security   (1) Casino "police." (2) The department that controls and protects the casino from crimes. (3) Protection of all people who are legitimately on the firm's property from bodily harm caused by the deliberate behavior of another person.

Security Monitor   A closed-circuit television monitor that allows employees to monitor security and safety throughout the property from a central location.

Self-Actualization   A psychological term referring to reaching one's ultimate potential through the use of personal skills and creative talents.

Self-Concept   A psychological term referring to the attitude a person holds toward him- or herself; for example, a person with a great deal of confidence in his abilities will be more likely to try new games such as moving from slots to the tables.

Self-Esteem Needs   A psychological term referring to a motivational need to feel good about oneself.

Semantic Differential   A rating scale that measures the respondent's reaction to some object or concept in terms of rating on bipolar scales defined with contrasting adjectives at each end.

Seniority   A term that refers to how long a person has been working for the company.

Sensor   A device that senses a specific change in its environment and transmits a signal so that some predetermined action can take place (e.g., a motion sensor can be used to detect any action in the money vault).

Sent It In   A gambling term referring to a bet against the house for large and/or frequent amounts of money.

Sequence   (1) In card playing, the order of rank in the cards. (2) In general, any chain of events and consequences.

Service   A type of product that is intangible; goods that are inseparable from the provider, variable in quality, and perishable.

Service Product   The entire bundle of tangibles and intangibles provided by a hospitality organization to guests during a service experience.

Service Quality   The difference between the service that the customer expects to get and the service that the customer actually receives.

Servicescape   The physical location and its characteristics within which the organization provides service to guests, especially the physical aspects of the setting that contribute to the guest's overall "feel" of the experience.

Seven-Out   In craps, rolling a seven after the initial throw, which becomes the shooter's losing point.

Seven Winner   In craps, a total of seven thrown by the shooter prior to her establishment of a pass-line point.

Sexual Harassment   A legal term referring to behavior marked by sexually suggestive remarks, unwanted touching and sexual advances, requests for sexual favors, or other verbal or physical conduct of a sexual nature.

Shade   A con artist's term for a cover or distraction for a scam.

Shading   A method of marking the backs of cards by delicately shading them with a dilute solution of marking ink, which is the same color as the ink already printed on the backs.

Shakeouts   According to product life cycle theory, when a product reaches its maturity age, there are too many competitors, thus a *shake-out* occurs that reduces the number, and only the strong survive.

Shape   A cheating technique that cuts down the die.

Shaping Behavior   A psychological term referring to systematically reinforcing each successive step that moves an individual closer to the desired response; for example, a person riding a bus to the casino is rewarded for getting on the bus with free twenty-dollar chips; she puts the chips into the slot machine and is rewarded with a payout; she puts her own money in and is rewarded with a payout.

Shark   (1) Any money loaner who charges exorbitant fees. (2) A skilled player who cheats.

Sharp   (1) Confident person. (2) Dapper or clothed in sartorial splendor.

Sharper   A card cheat or superior player who takes advantage of novices.

Shaved   A cheater's term for trimmed or altered dice.

Shell   An engineering term for the basic structural elements of a building, including the outside and supporting walls, foundation, frame, and roof.

Shield   In roulette, the glass surrounding the wheel that protects the public from flying balls.

Shift   Eight-hour workday.

Shift-Boss   In the casino management hierarchy, the person who controls the entire casino on his shift and answers only to the casino manager.

Shift the Cut   To secretly return the halves of a cut deck to their original position.

Shill   A casino term for an employee who sits down at an empty table and acts as a player to help get the game started.

Shimmy   Chemin de fer.

Shiner   A cheater's device; refers to a small mirror that reflects the face of the top card of the deck as it is dealt.

Shoe   In baccarat and blackjack, the container that stores the undealt cards.

Shoe Game   Either four- or six-deck blackjack using a shoe.

Shoot   In craps, a completed round in which the shooter makes or fails to make the point.

Shooter   In craps, a term referring to the player who is throwing the dice.

Shooting from the Hip   A slang expression that refers to making a decision spontaneously.

Shortage   An accounting term referring to when the total of cash and checks in the cash register drawer is less than the initial bank plus net cash receipts.

Shortcake   Shortchange.

Short Horn   In craps, small bet on the horn.

Shortpay   A payout made by a slot machine that is less than the amount indicated by the payout schedule; occurs when the hopper becomes depleted during a payout; the remaining amount is paid to the player by slot employees.

Short Shoe   In blackjack, the shoe with a number of cards removed from the decks used; alters the percentage against the players.

Shot   An illegal move by a player.

Showdown   In poker, after all bets are made, revealing the final hand.

Shuffle   In card games, the randomizing process of the cards before play starts.

Shuffle Check   When the dealer is done shuffling a shoe, some houses require a shuffle check: the dealer leaves the cards laced, and the floorperson approves the shuffle before the shoe is loaded.

Shuffle Tracking   In card games, the process by which a card player seeks to follow certain cards as they are shuffled in order to identify when they are likely to appear in the reshuffled deck.

Shy   (1) A slang term for owing money. (2) A slang term for being short on cash.

Shylock   An individual who loans money to players who are broke.

Shyster   Inexpensive, unscrupulous lawyer.

Sic-Bo   Oriental table game played with three dice; the objective is to select the individual numbers, or combination of numbers, that appear on the dice after they are shaken in a cup and exposed by the house dealer.

Side Bet   In craps, a bet made between players or onlookers for the results of a particular throw of the dice.

Side Game   A casino term for a less important and relatively lightly played game in a casino.

Silver   Silver dollars or one-dollar gaming tokens.

Silver Tongue   (1) High-class con man. (2) Convincing talker.

Simulcasting   The simultaneous transmission of sporting events providing the bettor with the opportunity to bet on more than one game, or race, at a time.

Single Action Numbers Bet   A bet on one digit.

Single-Deck   A blackjack game played with one deck (52 cards) and almost always handheld by the dealer.

Singles   One-dollar checks.

Single-0   (1) A con man's term for working alone. (2) In roulette, the single zero on the wheel.

Site Inspection   Previewing of a site (usually a convention center or hotel) to determine its suitability for the event/function/meeting being planned.

Six-Ace Flats   A gambling term for a pair of corrupted dice.

Sixaine   In roulette, the term for a six-number bet (two horizontal rows with three numbers each).

Sixes   In craps, a craps twelve that is when both die show six spots up.

Sixty Days   In craps, the six point.

Size   The numerical value of a card, disregarding the suit; primarily used in regard to marked cards.

Size-Into   A quick way of accounting at the table in which the dealer pushes a stack of cheques up to a shorter stack of cheques and takes the excess off so both stacks are equal.

Skimming   In embezzling, altering the accounting so that sums of money can be illegally taken "off the top" without knowledge.

Skinner   A cheat.

Skinny Dugan   In craps, a loser seven.

Sky   (1) A security term referring to the area above the main casino in which play is observed through one-way mirrors and video equipment. (2) A casino term referring to the employee(s) assigned to work in the sky area; short for eye-in-the-sky or casino surveillance.

Slambang   A gambling term for heavy, quick action.

Sleeper   (1) A gambling term referring to an unclaimed bet, wager, or part of a wager forgotten by a player. (2) A gambling term referring to a number that has not come up for a long time.

Slick Cup   A cheater's tool that is a dice cup with a polished inside surface to facilitate the effectiveness of loaded dice.

Slick Dice   A cheater's dice that have been altered to have smooth sides and rough sides.

Slickers   Professional gamblers.

Slide Shot   A dice mechanic's technique for controlling the roll of one or two dice.

Slot Booth   A booth in the slot area operated by a cashier who is responsible for making change for slot customers, redeeming coin, conducting hopper fill transactions, and making jackpot payouts.

Slot Drop   In casinos, the amount of coins collected in the bucket inside a cabinet underneath the slot machine.

Slot Handle   In casinos, the amount of money deposited into the machine by the customer.

Slots   An abbreviation for *slot machines,* which are the mechanical or computerized game machines.

Slot Win   The amount of win in the slot department for a given shift; usually recorded by amount and percentage of the coins dropped in the machines.

Slow Play   In poker, a strategic technique of placing a small bet as an opener, then if challenged, coming back with a large reraise.

Slow the Joint   To close down a gambling game or gambling house.

Slug   (1) In slot play, a cheater's false coin or chip. (2) In cards, a group of cards arranged by cheats for a desired result. (3) A cheater's device of a metal weight used to load dice.

Smack (the)   A gambling short con built around a game of matching coins.

Smacker   (1) One dollar. (2) A stupid person.

Smart   A gambler's term referring to someone who knows the score.

Smart Money   An intelligent gambler.

Snake-Eyes   In craps, a throw of two aces (ones).

Snapper   (1) In blackjack, a hand in which the first two cards are an ace and ten count, and pay one and a half times the bet. (2) A slang term for blackjack.

Sneak Pocket   A hidden pocket within the lining of the pants along the zipper used by a dice cheat to store dice.

Snowballs   Misspotted dice that bear only the numbers 4, 5, and 6.

Social Class   A sociological term referring to the relatively homogeneous divisions of society into which people are grouped based on similar lifestyles, values, norms, interests, and behaviors; for example, a casino that attracts the lower social class is more likely to have a majority of nickel slot machines rather than baccarat tables.

Social Needs   A psychological term referring to the motivational requirements that people have social interaction.

Social Responsibility   A term referring to the organization's obligation to be aware of its impact on the surrounding environment and to take appropriate actions.

Soft   Easy.

Soft Action (Soft Game)   A game composed of players with limited gambling knowledge who are, therefore, particularly easy to cheat.

Soft Count   In casinos, counting the value of paper-like dollar bills, cheques, markers, and so on.

Soft-Count Room   The location where the drop boxes are stored prior to the soft count and where the actual counting of the drop box contents takes place; a highly secured area under constant video surveillance monitoring.

Soft Hand   In blackjack, a hand with an ace that can be valued as one or eleven.

Soft Opening   In hotels and other similar facilities, when the property opens for business prior to the official opening in order to smooth out operations.

Solid   Trustworthy, good.

Sommelier   In a restaurant, the person with considerable wine knowledge who orders and serves wines.

SOP   An abbreviation for *standard operating procedure.*

97

Sovereign Nation   In Native American tribes, a federal status indicating that they are a separate body from Americans and as such, they are exempt from state betting limits or taxation.

Spa   A type of hotel or resort that provides hot springs, baths, or other health and fitness facilities, and services.

Span of Control   A management term referring to the number of subordinates reporting directly to a superior.

Specifications   An engineering term referring to the descriptions and directions that accompany blueprints.

Spell   In craps, a term referring to a similar sequence of passes.

Spill   When a dice mechanic accidentally drops one or both palmed dice so that more than two dice are in evidence at one time.

Spin   In roulette, a term referring to setting the wheel in play.

Spindle   In roulette, a metal piece that attaches the roulette wheel to the hub.

Spin Them   In craps, an attempt to control the dice.

Spit   Gambling term referring to a player's very small bankroll.

Splash Move   Ploy by gambling cheats who run through a cheating method without actually doing it to see if any suspicions are aroused.

Splinters   Individual player, arriving independently or on a junket, who are brought in by the casino to gamble.

Split   In blackjack, a pair that can be split into two hands as long as the same amount is bet on each hand, as in a player who *splits*, draws cards for both hands.

Split Bet   Bet on two numbers.

Splitter   A cheater's term referring to a substitute gaffed die that is interchanged for one of a pair of dice to change the outcome.

Splitting Pairs   In blackjack, when two of a kind can be turned into two separate hands.

Spook   A cheating term referring to a person who reads the dealer's hole card.

Spooking   A cheating maneuver in which a team of cheats reads the dealer's hole card and bets accordingly.

Spooning   In slot machines, a cheating device that is spoon-shaped and used to bring about a payoff.

Sports Pool   A business that accepts wagers on events with the exception of horse and other race events.

Spot   Slang term referring to someone who discovers a deviation.

Spot Card   Any card ranked from ace to ten.

Spots   (1) The area printed on the felt layout designating where the bets are to be placed. (2) In keno, the numbers a player marks on a card.

Spread   When a player bets more than one hand simultaneously.

Spreadsheet   A software package that allows the user to turn a computer's memory into a large worksheet in which data and formulas can be entered to perform a variety of calculations.

Spread Your Deck   A casino expression referring to a dealer gathering up all the cards and spreading them in a smooth arc in the middle of the table.

Spring   (1) Slang for getting a person released from police custody. (2) A slang expression for someone to pick up the tab.

Square   (1) In roulette, a bet on four connected numbers. (2) A slang expression for a conservative individual who is not in fashion.

Square a Beef   A slang expression that means to resolve a gripe.

Square It   A slang expression in which a person corrects a wrong.

Squares   Any honest gambling equipment.

Squawker   Loud, habitual complainer.

Squeeze   (1) Cheating device. (2) To control or coerce.

Squeeze Play   A method of playing a slot machine without depositing a coin by squeezing the handle inward as it is pulled down so that it goes around the locking mechanism, which is normally released only when a coin is inserted.

Stack   A column of twenty cheques or coins.

Stake   (1) A wager. (2) The money to be bet on a series of gambles.

Stacked Deck   A cheating term that refers to a pack of cards that have been prearranged to suit a specific purpose.

Stakeholders   A management term referring to any constituency in the environment that is affected by an organization's decision and policies (e.g., two types of stakeholders for a casino can be the employees and stockholders).

Stakes   A gambling term referring to the amount wagered.

Stand   A blackjack term referring to a player's decision not to draw additional cards.

Stand Alone   A management term for something that can be separated from the whole and still function efficiently, as in a hotel can be a *stand alone* division, or it can be used as part of the casino effort as an amenity.

Standard Deviation (1) A commonly used measure of variability whose size indicates the dispersion of a distribution. (2) A mathematical concept referring to the spread of results around an expected point.

Standard Hours A management term referring to the amount of time in which a given, well-defined procedure should be accomplished.

Standoff A tie.

Standard Operating Procedures (SOP) A management term referring to the traditional ways that operations are done; often dictated by the corporate headquarters.

Standards Levels of expected performance.

Stand-Up Person Trustworthy.

Status Symbol In consumer behavior, tangible evidence of an individual's social position.

Stay A player's indication to the dealer that no more cards are desired on a hand.

Steam Heavy surveillance.

Steamer A player on a losing streak who increases the size of his bets in an effort to recoup his losses.

Steaming A player's strategy of increasing the bet after each losing hand during a losing streak.

Steerer A scam artist who finds suckers to come to a steer joint.

Steer Joint Crooked casino.

Stereotyping A psychological term referring to the tendency to judge a person on the basis of one's perception of a group, such as race or age.

Stewarding The department in a hotel or food-service operation responsible for the back of the house: cleanliness in the food and beverage areas, the cleanliness of the china, cutlery, glassware, and the customer of related food and beverage equipment.

Stick In craps, the hockey stick-like device the dealer uses to retrieve the dice from across the table to return them to the shooter.

Stickman In craps, the dealer who stands directly across from the boxman, calls the game, and controls its pace; she uses a hooked stick to retrieve the dice and push them toward the shooter.

Stiff (1) A gambling term referring to a winning gambler who does not toke (tip) the dealer. (2) In blackjack, a hand that has a small chance of winning (twelve to sixteen points). (3) Someone who does not bet for dealers.

Stiffed   Slang for a person who receives no tip for providing services, such as a dealer or a server.

Stiff Hand   In blackjack, a difficult hand that has a total of twelve to sixteen and may bust if an additional card is drawn.

Stiff Sheet   The form used to record the opening table inventory, closing table inventory, drop, fills, credits, markers, and gross revenue/win for each table game by shift; completed during the soft-count process.

Sting   (1) A cheater's term for when the con man gets the money. (2) Law enforcement term for a covert action.

Stock   A casino term referring to the portion of an undealt deck of cards that may be used later during the same deal.

Stonewall Jackson   Miser.

Store   Slang term for a casino.

Store Dice   Imperfect cubes or dice.

Storm   A gambler's term for a statistically significant deviation from the average.

Straddle   In poker, a bet of twice the ante placed by the second player before the deal.

Straight   In poker, a hand of any five cards in numerical sequence.

Straighten Up Your Rack   A casino expression said to a dealer indicating that he should arrange the racked silver and cheques into regulation stacks so that the floorperson can quickly count from a distance.

Straight Flush   In poker, any five cards in numerical sequence and the same suit.

Straight Ticket   In keno, a simple ticket with no combination bets.

Straight-Up Bet   In roulette, a bet on a single number.

Strategic Business Unit (SBU)   A management term referring to a structural group within a firm that has some autonomy.

Streak   A gambling term referring to a series of wins or losses.

Street Bet   In roulette, a bet on a row of three numbers across.

Stress   A generic term referring to the mobilization of the body's energy sources when confronted with demands or conflict.

Strike (the)   A cheating, or second dealing, technique in which the top card is pushed over slightly so as to expose the outer corner of the second card that is then dealt out by the thumb.

Strike Number   For card counters, the strategic number that alters the betting.

Stringing In slots, a cheating technique in which a cheat inserts a coin on a string and pulls it back out of the machine.

Strip A universal term for the casino row along Las Vegas Boulevard (*Las Vegas Strip*).

Strippers A cheater's device that refers to a deck of cards whose edges have been trimmed.

Strip The Deck A cheating method of shuffling that consists of dropping a few cards at a time off the top of the deck.

Strong Effective cheating move.

Strong Arm Physical coercion.

Strong Work Crooked cards marked with heavy lines.

Stuck Lose.

Stud Poker In poker, a game in which some of the cards are dealt face up and others face down.

Stuffed Person with plenty of cash.

Sub A cheating technique in which a concealed pocket or other device on the clothing or body is used for holding illegally taken cheques.

Sucker Gullible person.

Sucker Bet A gambling term referring to a bet that has a high probability of losing.

Sucker Word Cheating terms used only by noncheaters.

Sucker Work Ineffective gaffs sold to amateurs who do not know any better.

Suction Dice Dice with concave surfaces.

Suite In a hotel, one or more bedrooms connected to a parlor or living room.

Suite Hotel A type of hotel whose guestrooms have a separate bedroom and living spaces and sometimes a kitchenette.

Super George In dealer's jargon, a player who bets a lot for the dealer.

Sure Thing Any bet that has very little chance of losing.

Surrender In blackjack, to give up on a bad hand and lose half the bet.

Surveillance The ability of the organization to observe all behaviors on the total area of the property.

Survey A research tool in which information is systematically gathered.

Sweat   (1) To worry about. (2) The term used to describe a boss who is worried if the house is losing money.

Sweat Card   A plastic card placed near the end of the deck by the dealer to indicate the point at which the cards will be reshuffled.

Sweater   A casino term for a person who only watches a game.

Sweep   A casino term for clearing the chips off the table.

Sweeten a Bet   Legally adding checks to a wager before the cards have been dealt.

Swinging   A casino term for stealing by a casino employee.

Swing Shift   Shift from six or seven p.m. to two or three a.m.

Switch   A con technique for illegally exchanging one object for another.

Switching   (1) The process of transferring the mark's interest from the come-on proposition to the deal that actually constitutes the con. (2) The process of transferring the mark's confidence from the outside man to the inside man in a big con.

SWOT   A strategic planning term for the analysis of an organization's *strengths* and *weaknesses* against the environmental *opportunities* and *threats*.

System   Any strategic method using a mathematical calculation of chances.

System Bettor   Any player using a system to bet.

Systems Approach   A management theory that sees an organization as a set of interrelated and interdependent parts.

T

Table Bankroll   In blackjack, the chips in the tray at a specific table.

Table Card   For premium players wagering through the use of call bets, the table card is a form used to track player wins and losses until the end of the period of play. When complete, any amount owed by the player will be settled to a marker and the marker number will be indicated on the table card as a reference; also referred to as an *auxiliary table card*, *player card*, or a *call-bet sheet*.

Table Credits   The transfer of chips, tokens, and/or coin from a specific table game to the casino cage; also used to transfer an unpaid gaming marker to the casino cage.

Table Drop   (1) In casinos, the amount of money, and markers, that are placed into the drop box at a gaming table. (2) In casinos, the amount of money that a customer exchanges; cash for chips.

Table Fills   The transfer of chips, tokens, and/or coin from the casino cage to a specific gaming table.

Table Float   The inventory of cheques maintained on a table in a tray that is secured by a clear, lockable cover when the table is not in use.

Table Game   A game that uses a table as part of the action.

Table Game Drop   The process of removing the drop box from each gaming table at the end of the designated gaming shift and replacing that box with an empty box for the next shift; also includes the security and transportation of the removed drop boxes from the pit area to the soft count room.

Table Hopping   A gambling term for a person who switches gaming tables in an attempt to change her luck.

Table Inventory   The supply of chips, tokens, and coin stored on a gaming table that are used by the dealer to pay off winning player bets, store losing player bets, and exchange chips for currency.

Table Inventory Slip (TIS)   The accounting document that records the monetary amount of checks that are in each table game rack at the end of each shift or when a game is closed.

Table Limit   A casino term for the maximum and minimum bets allowed at a table.

Table Stakes   In poker, a method of placing a maximum betting limit on wagers.

Table Win   In casinos, this amount is calculated by subtracting the value of the chips missing from the bankroll of the table from the drop.

T-Account   In accounting, a two-column system in which charges are posted on the left side and payments on the right side.

Take   (1) A gaming expression for the casino receipts. (2) Slang for accepting a bribe. (3) Depart.

Take a Bath   To lose heavily or to go broke.

Take and Pay   A casino term referring to the dealer's method of settling up with the winners and losers.

Take an Edge   In gaming, to acquire a dishonest advantage.

Take Down   In gaming, to remove a bet (usually pertains to a bet for the dealers).

Take It   A craps term for backing the dice to win by taking the odds.

Take It Off from the Inside   Employee theft.

Take It Off the Top   A payout before any disbursements are made.

Take Me Down   In craps, an instruction from a player to the dealer meaning, "remove my bet(s)."

Take-Off Man   Partner from a cheating scam who makes the large wagers.

Take-Off Pad   Place at the front base of the shoe where the cards are drawn.

Take the Odds   In craps, to accept a "wrong" bet at odds.

Taking the Count   In casinos, the pit boss may stop the action at a table so that security guards can do a cash inventory.

Tall Organization   Organization that has numerous hierarchical levels and narrow spans of control.

Tap Out   Lose one's total bank or money.

Tappers   Dice with an inside shifting weight.

Target Market   A large, easily identifiable, and accessible group of people who have common interests so that a company can sell to them.

Tariff   Published fares, rates, charges, and/or related conditions.

Task Force   Temporary joining of personnel from different organizational subunits to accomplish a specific, well-defined, complex task.

Task Significance   The degree to which the job has an important impact on the organization.

Tat   Con game using dice with only high numbers.

Tear Up   Pretending to tear up a check from a mark and then cashing it.

Technical Skill   Specific knowledge of and ability to perform specific tasks and duties.

Technology   Major techniques or tasks performed to produce the output of an organization.

Tees   Misspotted dice that have certain numbers repeated on opposite sides whereas other numbers have been left off entirely.

Telegraph   Nonverbal action that betrays intentions to others, such as security.

Tell   In poker, a nervous reaction by a player that signals his cards.

Tellas Consent Decree   In 1981, the EEOC won a discrimination suit against twenty Las Vegas hotels, which opened dealer opportunities to women and minorities, resulting in the setting of hiring quotas.

Tell the Tale   For a con man, usually the inside man, to explain to the mark the deal by which she is supposed to profit.

Ten Rich   High number of ten count cards remaining in the deck according to a card counter.

Ten-Stop Machine   A gaffed slot machine that has twenty symbols on each of its reels but is gaffed so that only ten of them can appear on its pay line.

Terminal   The keyboard and monitor for a computer system.

The Ming   The organization and presentation of the guest experience around a unifying idea or theme, often a fantasy theme, to give guests the illusion of being in a place and time other than "the here and now."

Theoretical Hold   In slots, the intended hold percentage or win as computed by reference to its payout schedule and reel strip settings; deviation of the actual hold percentage from the theoretical hold percentage can be an indication of problems.

Theoretical Hold Worksheet   A worksheet provided by the manufacturer for all slot machines, which indicates the theoretical percentages that the slot machine should hold based on adequate levels of coin-in; also indicates the reel strip setting, number of coins that may be played, the payout schedule, the number of reels, and other information descriptive of the particular type of slot machine; also known as a *spec sheet*.

Theory X   Traditional view of motivation that assumes employees must be closely supervised and controlled.

Theory Y   Theory of motivation that assumes employees are self-motivated and can be delegated authority.

Theory Z   Motivation theory that suggests that employees should be given a participatory role in defining their jobs and in decision making.

There's Work Down   Crooked dice are being used.

They're Burning Up   Dice that make pass after pass.

Thin One   Dime.

Third Base   (1) Far left-hand seat on the blackjack table. (2) Last hand dealt.

Third Dozen   In roulette, a bet on the numbers twenty-five through thirty-six.

Three-Card Monte   A three-card game; the object is to pick one of three cards down that is the queen and avoid picking any aces.

Three-Number Bet   In roulette, a bet paying eleven to one.

Three of a Kind   In poker, three cards of the same number.

Three-Way Craps   In craps, when one player bets equal amounts on two, three, and twelve separately, yet concurrently.

Thumb Out   Process of using the thumb of the hand holding a stack to equalize a series of stacks of cheques.

Ticket   Bar-coded slip of paper used in place of money or coins in slot machines.

Tie   Hand in which both the player and dealer hold the same total value.

Tie-Up   Person who keeps the mark interested in the scam until the end.

Tight   (1) Little known cheating technique. (2) Hustler who can keep a secret.

Tightwad   Miserly or stingy person.

Time-and-a-Half   (1) When a player has blackjack, dealer pays one and one-half times the bet. (2) Overtime pay.

Time and Motion Study   Process of analyzing jobs to determine the best movements for performing each task; for example, watching dealers to eliminate any superfluous moves so that play can be faster.

Time Management   Scheduling time effectively.

Tip   To reveal cheating secrets.

TIPS   Standards for *training for intervention procedures* by servers; sponsored by the NRA, TIPS is a certification program that informs participants about alcohol and the effects of alcohol on people, the common signs of intoxication, and how to help customers avoid drinking too much.

Title VII   In employment, the portion of the 1964 Civil Rights Act that prohibits discrimination in hiring and promoting.

Toilet   Term for casino.

Toke Box   A slotted, locked box for tips.

Toke Committee   The dealers who are elected to represent each shift when interpreting the rules and addressing problems.

Toke Cutters   The group of dealers who are voted by their shifts to count and divide the daily tokes into individual shares; they are given extra money for this duty and are responsible for the money.

Tokens   Substitutes for coins; produced so that they are unique to each casino and are used for slot machine play, primarily in machines with denominations of one dollar or more.

Toke Rules   A list of rules established by the dealers, or the house, as to how the tokens are to be divided.

Tokes   Tips, gratuity.

Toke Split   Pooling and distributing all tips to all dealers.

Tom   Player who leaves little or no tip.

Tools   Altered dice that cheaters use.

Top   Upper level management or reputable information source.

Topping the Deck   Cheater who palms off the top of the deck on the cut.

Tops   A die that has duplicate numbers.

Tops and Bottoms   Gaffed dice that bear only three different numbers on each die.

Total Quality Management (TQM)   Philosophy of management that is driven by customer needs and expectations.

Touch   (1) To ask for a loan. (2) Money obtained by cheating.

Tour-Basing Fare   Special reduced, round-trip fare with date and time restrictions.

Tourism   Industry that caters to travelers and includes travel, hotels, transportation, and so on.

Tourneur   In European roulette, the dealer who spins the wheel and throws the ball into the wheel runway.

Tour Operator   Company that specializes in the planning and operation of prepaid, preplanned vacations.

Tour Organizer   Individual who organizes tours for special groups of people.

Tour Package   Travel plan that includes elements of a vacation like transportation and accommodations.

Tour Wholesaler   Company that plans, markets, and operates tours to intermediaries but rarely to the end user.

Tout   (1) To ask for bets. (2) Verbally promote a game.

TQM   An abbreviation for *total quality management*.

Trade Show   Events where all, or part, of the industry (suppliers, carriers, intermediaries, and destination marketing organizations) is brought together to share information and sell their products.

Training   Learning process whereby people acquire skills, or knowledge, to aid in the achievement of goals.

Transversale Plein   In roulette, a three-number bet on a horizontal row.

Trap   Bet that is not what it appears to be.

Tray   In casinos, a specific area for handling chips.

Trey   In craps, three on a die.

Trim   To defraud someone.

Trip Dice   Trimmed edges on a pair of dice.

Trip Work   Altered dice that have some edges extended slightly to prevent them from rolling over those edges.

True Count   Running count adjusted for the number of cards or decks remaining to be played.

Try-Out   Interview audition done in front of supervisors.

T-Test   A hypothesis test that uses the t-statistic and the t-distribution to determine whether to reject or retain the null hypothesis.

Tub   Wheel.

Tumble   Discover a scam.

Turkey   (1) Ignorant blackjack player. (2) Any player who is unpleasant to deal to.

Turn a Sucker   Convince a mark to help con others.

Turnover   (1) Process of employees leaving an organization and being replaced. (2) The number of times the seats or tables in a restaurant are used in a given period (day).

Twenty-One   Alternate name for blackjack.

Twinkle   Hidden mirror that allows a dealer to see the cards as he deals.

Two Bits   Twenty-five cents.

Two-Card Push Off   A cheating, or second dealing, technique in which the top two cards are slid over (together) in alignment and the second card is pulled out as the top card is drawn back onto the deck.

Twofer   In blackjack, $2.50 chip.

Two-Number Bet   In craps, a bet that one of two specific numbers will, or will not, be thrown before a seven.

Two Pairs   In poker, two cards of one value and two of another value.

Two-Roll Bet   In craps, a bet decided by the next two throws.

Two-Way Bet   Bet between player and dealer in which winnings are divided equally.

Type-A Behavior   Behavior marked by a chronic sense of time urgency and an excessive competitive drive.

Type-B Behavior   Behavior that is relaxed, easygoing, and noncompetitive.

U

Uncertainty   Situation in which the decision maker does not have a clear probability estimate of the outcomes.

Underground Economy   Unreported economic activity (e.g., illegal gambling).

Under the Gun   (1) In poker, a player who must bet first. (2) In card games, the player to the left of the dealer.

Unemployment   (1) In economics, workers who would be willing to work at prevailing wages but cannot find jobs. (2) In the U.S. Bureau of Labor Statistics, a worker who is unemployed, is not working, and either waiting for recall from layoff or has actively looked for work in the previous four weeks.

Uniform System of Accounts   A system of accounts used in the hospitality industry whereby all accounts have shared codes and all accounting procedures are done the same way.

Union   A formal association of workers that promotes the welfare of its members, such as the Teamster's Union.

Unit   Measure used by gamblers to set the size of their wagers, usually based on the minimum bet at a particular game.

Unpaid Shill   Steady low roller.

Up a Tree   Dealer's face-up card.

Up-card   In blackjack, a dealer's card dealt face up.

Utility   In economics, the satisfaction derived from the consumption of a commodity.

V

Validity   Research term used to reflect the extent to which differences in scores reflect true differences among individuals, groups, or situations.

Valence   Strength of the valuation of a reward.

Value-for-Money Bet   Bet in which the true probability of a result is greater than the odds being offered against the result.

Variable Costs   Expenses that change directly with sales volume.

Variance   Difference between expected and actual outcomes, expressed numerically.

Velvet   Winnings.

Vertical Marketing System   Integration of all the levels of manufacturers, wholesalers, and retailers who cooperate to sell a product.

Vic   Victim or mark.

Video Lotteries   Lotteries played on computerized terminals; allow the winner instant verification of win or loss.

Vig   An abbreviation for *vigorish*.

Vigorish   (1) A 5 percent commission charged by the house for certain bets. (2) House edge.

W

Walk   (1) Player who leaves a gaming table. (2) A guest the hotel turns away due to a lack of rooms.

Walked With   An expression referring to the amount of table cheques a player leaves the table with.

Walk-In   A person who requests a hotel room without a reservation.

Walking Money   Money given by a casino to a player who has lost all of her funds in order to return home.

Walking on His Heels   Dazed.

Want   A need shaped by a person's knowledge, culture, and personality.

Wash   Breaking even.

Washing the Cards   Combining several decks of cards prior to shuffling by mixing them together on the table in random fashion.

Wave   To bend the edge of a card during play for identification purposes.

Way Bet   In keno, a ticket marked to combine number bets in various ways.

Way Off   Defective.

Weed   Palm or remove bills while handling money.

Weigh Count   The dollar amount of coins and tokens removed from the slot machine drop buckets and counted by the hard-count team through the use of a weight scale.

Weigh Wrap Verification   The process of comparing, by denomination, the total value of the weight to the total value of the wrapped coins and racked tokens; significant differences between the weight and the wrap are investigated and noted.

Weight   Cheater jargon for loaded dice.

Well-Heeled   Sophisticated.

Welsh   Failure to pay a gambling debt.

Welter   Gambler who fails to pay off his gambling losses.

Whale   Term used by casino employees to describe a big bettor (e.g., a gambler with a credit line in excess of $50 thousand dollars).

Wheel   Roulette wheel or game.

Wheel Roller   Roulette dealer.

Whip Cup   Cheater's dice cup with inner surface polished.

Whip Shot   A controlled dice shot in which the two dice are spun from the hand and strike the table surface with a flat spinning motion so that the controlled numbers are on top when the dice stop.

Whirl   In craps, a bet covering seven and the horn numbers in five equal amounts.

Whistle Blowing   Employees who report fraudulent or wasteful organizational activities to appropriate authorities.

White on White   Marked cards with small white markings on white border.

Whites   One dollar.

Whiz Machines   A machine used for dispensing and controlling manual slips used for table fills, table credits, slot hopper fills, and slot jackpot payouts; the supply of slips contained in the machine is usually in triplicate, with one copy remaining in a secured compartment within the machine once the slips are dispensed; primarily used as a backup in the event of computer failure.

Wide Open   A lot of fast moving game action.

Wild Card   Card(s) given the power to substitute for other cards in suit and value.

Win   The amount of each dollar wagered that is won or held by the house before operating expenses and other costs have been paid and does not represent profit.

Windfall   An unexpected large influx of money.

Window   A cheater's term for location where dealer's whole card can be seen.

Wire   (1) Sign used between players. (2) In slots, a device used to rig a payout. (3) Secretly worn tape recorder.

Wired   In blackjack, a good hand.

Wire Joint   Corrupt gambling house in which tables are rigged or dice are magnetized.

Wireman   In slots, a cheat who slips a wire into a drilled hole in the machine to control the spinning wheels.

Won't Bite   Will not take the risk.

Won't Spring   Will not pay the bill for others.

Wood   Nonplayer.

Word of Mouth   Information about a service experience passed orally from past (and other social information sources) to potential customers.

Work   (1) Deformed dice. (2) Process of changing the dice.

Workforce Diversity   Employees in organizations are heterogeneous in terms of gender, race, ethnicity, or other characteristics.

Working Bets   In craps, all money or chips that are riding on the next roll of the dice.

Working Stack   In craps, stacks of checks directly in front of a base dealer used for making payoffs.

Work Teams   Groups of individuals that cooperate in completing a set of tasks.

World-Class Service   Level of service that stresses personal attention to each guest.

Worst of It   Disadvantage.

Wrap   The dollar amount of coins and tokens removed from the slot machine drop buckets and wrapped by the hard-count team.

Write   The total amount wagered in the race book, sports book, keno, and bingo.

Writer   An employee of the race book, sports book, or keno who writes tickets.

Wrong Bettor   In craps, a player who bets against the shooter by placing the don't come or don't pass bet.

Y

Yard   One hundred dollars.

Yield Management   A revenue management approach used to maximize the sales of perishable inventories by controlling prices and capacity.

Yo   The number eleven on a crap game; if bet on a one-roll proposition bet, then it pays fifteen to one.

Z

Zero   The thirty-seventh number on a roulette wheel.

Zero-Base Budgeting   System in which budget requests start from zero regardless of previous appropriations.

Zero Out   Settle the account in full.

Zombie   Gambler who hides any outward emotion.

Zoom   In security, a camera with the capacity to magnify the image.

Zukes   Gratuities or tips.